Immigrant Exclusion and Insecurity in Africa
Coethnic Strangers

This book explores the diverse immigrant experiences in urban West Africa, where some groups integrate seamlessly while others face exclusion and violence. It shows, counterintuitively, that cultural similarities between immigrants and their hosts do not help immigrant integration and may, in fact, disrupt it. This book is one of the first to describe and explain in a systematic way immigrant integration in the developing world, where half of all international migrants go. It relies on intensive fieldwork tracking two immigrant groups in three host cities and draws from in-depth interviews and survey data to paint a picture of the immigrant experience from both immigrant and host perspectives.

Claire L. Adida is Assistant Professor of Political Science at the University of California, San Diego, where she is also a faculty affiliate with the Center for Comparative Immigration Studies and with the Policy Design and Evaluation Lab. Her work has been published in the *Proceedings of the National Academy of Sciences*, *Comparative Political Studies*, and *Economics and Politics*. Her research applies experimental, survey, and interview methods to the study of ethnic politics. Adida's fieldwork has taken her to Nigeria, Niger, Benin, Ghana, Uganda, and South Africa.

Immigrant Exclusion and Insecurity in Africa

Coethnic Strangers

CLAIRE L. ADIDA
University of California, San Diego

CAMBRIDGE
UNIVERSITY PRESS

CAMBRIDGE
UNIVERSITY PRESS

32 Avenue of the Americas, New York, NY 10013-2473, USA

Cambridge University Press is part of the University of Cambridge.

It furthers the University's mission by disseminating knowledge in the pursuit of education, learning, and research at the highest international levels of excellence.

www.cambridge.org
Information on this title: www.cambridge.org/9781107047723

© Claire L. Adida 2014

First published 2014

Printed in the United States of America

A catalog record for this publication is available from the British Library.

Library of Congress Cataloging in Publication Data
Adida, Claire L., 1979– author.
Immigrant exclusion and insecurity in Africa / Claire L. Adida.
    pages   cm
Includes bibliographical references and index.
ISBN 978-1-107-04772-3 (hardback) – ISBN 978-1-107-65056-5 (pbk.)
1. Africa, West – Emigration and immigration.   2. Africa, West – Emigration and immigration – Government policy.   3. Immigrants – Africa, West – Social conditions.   4. Africa, West – Ethnic relations.   5. Rural-urban migration – Africa, West.   I. Title.
JV9020.A35   2014
304.8'66–dc23   2013037761

ISBN 978-1-107-04772-3 Hardback

For Jen, Gabi, and Mina; in memory of Chief Olujobi.

Contents

List of Figures

List of Tables

Acknowledgments

The idea for this book germinated during a research trip to East Africa in 2005. I was a graduate assistant on a project on coethnicity in Uganda at the time. In the mornings, I enjoyed the luxury of reading the local newspapers while sipping Nescafé in a house overlooking Lake Victoria (subsequent fieldwork would never be as luxurious again); on a regular basis, anti-Asian incidents sprinkled the pages of the *Daily Monitor* and *New Vision*. This piqued my interest, and I began reading about Idi Amin's expulsion of Uganda's more than 50,000 Asians in 1972. Although this event attracted significant media attention, I soon discovered that a myriad other less-publicized expulsion events had occurred throughout sub-Saharan Africa since the 1960s. Clearly, anti-immigrant politics were alive and well in a region typically known for sending migrants elsewhere, not for hosting them.

And yet, systematic research on immigrant exclusion in Africa offered a rather desolate landscape. I saw in that a research opportunity, which – eight years later – has culminated into this book. With it I try to make a dent into our understanding of the immigrant experience in urban Africa. My approach has been to immerse myself into two migrant communities in three West African urban centers and to draw insights from the local dynamics I witnessed and that have been recounted to me in interviews and surveys. As a result, I owe countless individual immigrants, who remain anonymous throughout this project, an immense debt of gratitude: these immigrants shared with me their time, their stories, and some shade in their market stall. Without their kindness and generosity, this project would not have come to fruition. The community leaders I befriended took me in and provided the necessary introductions to jump-start my data collection. Jide Ogunleke in Accra and Chief Olujobi in Cotonou, in particular, were uniquely generous with their time and attention to my project.

A team of fantastic local research assistants ensured the successful execution of six different surveys in three different cities: I am thankful to Jide Ogunleke and Abdul Barki Moses in Accra; Chief Olujobi and his team in Cotonou; and Mansoor in Niamey. I also relied countless times on the openness and generosity of friends and colleagues in the field: Mike Ajani, Kofi Anani, Professor John K. Anarfi, Pastor Ezekiel Aremu, Daniel Asare, Dominic and Ester Ayine, James Bot, Moumouni Chabi Sikka, Professor John Igué, John Metchie, Al-Haji Musa Baba, and finally Awo and Bob, Soglo, Nana and Abdou, Doris and Dan, Romeo Gansey and Fabien Vidal.

At Stanford University, where I pursued most of this research, I benefited from the advice and guidance of my dissertation committee: David Laitin, Jeremy Weinstein, James Fearon, and Doug McAdam. I was lucky to work with a team of inspiring, supportive, and demanding advisors who taught me to think like a social scientist. Their feedback throughout my graduate career, and especially during my fieldwork year, was instrumental to this project. In particular, I am grateful to David Laitin, who offered an endless supply of inspiration and motivation through his own work and unwavering passion for this discipline; and to Doug McAdam, who never let me rest on my laurels once the dissertation was completed. His enthusiasm and support were key to turning the dissertation into a book. Lew Bateman, senior editor at Cambridge University Press, believed in this book project from the start and guided me ever so patiently through the review and publication process.

This project also benefited from the critical eye and helpful feedback of friends and colleagues at Stanford and UCSD. Leonardo Arriola, Rikhil Bhavnani, John Bullock, Jowei Chen, Dara Cohen, Rafaela Dancygier, Scott Desposato, Jesse Driscoll, Roy Elis, Karen Ferree, Desha Girod, Laurel Harbridge, Kimuli Kasara, Alex Kuo, Bethany Lacina, Yotam Margalit, Sam Popkin, Natan Sachs, Alex Scacco, Jed Stiglitz, Jeremy Wallace, and Jessica Weeks afforded me their time and piece of mind. Desha Girod, in particular, saw this project grow from the very beginning, and helped me figure out my "story" on countless paper napkins in the coffee shops of San Francisco. Matt Nanes and Kate Blackwell provided critical research assistance in the last stages of production.

My family provided intellectual and emotional support throughout. My parents, Pierre and Yvette Adida, opened countless doors for me over the years. My conversations with my sister, Juliette Adida, taught me to think more creatively; those with my brother, Benjamin Adida, taught me to think more analytically.

My life partner, Jennifer Burney, has seen this project from beginning to end, from muddled research ideas to taxing fieldwork, from the ebb and flow of writing to the ups and downs of publishing. She has been there every step of the way. She and our two beautiful children, Gabriel and Mina, are my foundation: this book is for them.

1

Introduction

1.1 A Tale of Two Families

"They will kill you, so go!" Mary exclaimed as she recounted to me the events of November 1969, when she and her family were forced to leave Ghana – her birth country – and return to Ogbomosho, Nigeria.[1] Mary was born in 1941 in Tamale, the capital of Ghana's Northern Region. Mary belongs to the Yoruba ethnic group, a group indigenous to land now located mostly in Nigeria and Benin. She has lived and worked as a petty merchant in Ghana's urban centers most of her life. A trading opportunity originally brought her parents to northern Ghana from Ogbomosho, as it did many other members of Nigeria's Yoruba community.

Mary lived a rather typical Yoruba existence in Ghana: her parents sent her back to Nigeria to attend primary school and learn the Yoruba language, but she quickly returned to Ghana upon completing her primary education. She met her husband through the Yoruba First Baptist Church of Tamale, a vibrant church where the Yoruba-only membership prays and sings in Yoruba. Soon after marrying, she and her husband moved to

---

[1] Interview, Accra, Ghana: February 6(A), 2007. The letter "A" denotes the first interview conducted that day. "Mary" is a pseudonym used to protect the anonymity of the respondent.

Kumasi, the capital of Ghana's coffee-producing Ashanti Region, home to the historically powerful Ashanti Kingdom. There they rented a house from a fellow Yoruba they met in the Yoruba First Baptist Church of Kumasi. Mary's husband provided some start-up funds and she began her career as a petty trader in Kumasi. She joined her hometown union, the Ogbomosho Parapo, and regularly remitted money back to Ogbomosho through the organization to support hospitals and orphanages.

Mary was twenty eight years old when Prime Minister Busia of Ghana decreed his famous Alien Compliance Order on November 18, 1969. This executive order announced over the radio that "it has come to the notice of the Ghana government that some aliens are residing in Ghana without the proper documents. The government is hereby giving them two weeks to regularize their stay in Ghana or they will be expelled."[2] Mary recalls with slight amusement how she first thought that Prime Minister Busia was joking. But when Ghanaians began harassing her and her family, she realized this was no joke: "You don't know whether they will kill you or they will not kill you. . . . All of us – we are afraid!" The Kumasi she knew turned into an unwelcoming and unsafe space. An official countdown to the December deadline was aired on the radio everyday, and as Ghanaian police patrolled the streets to ensure Ghana's "aliens" were packing up their belongings, fear overtook Ghana's Yoruba community. Mary's husband rented a car to Lagos; they left with her child and parents promptly before the December deadline.

Mary might have been a Yoruba, an ethnic group indigenous to Nigeria, but she was born in Ghana. She had a Ghanaian birth certificate. She owned indigenous Ashanti dress. She spoke fluent Twi, the Ashanti language. Her parents owned a house in Tamale. And yet none of these factors protected her during the bushfire that was Busia's Alien Compliance Order. Her parents were forced to undersell their house, and her entire family followed the exodus back to Nigeria, a country she did not know. Many died on the road back. As Mary recalls, "it was no small thing."

---

[2] Interview with a Yoruba Muslim chief in Accra, Ghana: January 24(B), 2007.

Sulaiman assures me that there is no such thing as a Ghanaian Hausa: "Most of us who were born here...our grand-fathers came from Nigeria."[3] Sulaiman is a Hausa born in Ghana. The Hausa, an ethnic group indigenous to land now located in northern Nigeria and Niger, have become such a natural part of Ghana's demographic landscape that the debate as to whether Ghanaian Hausas exist, and whether Hausa is an indigenous Ghanaian language, is current and vivid.[4] Sulaiman was born in 1948 in Ghana, but he says he is originally from Nigeria: his parents migrated as traders from Nigeria to Accra, Ghana's capital city.

Although Sulaiman has married a woman who shares his religion, Islam, his wife is a Yoruba born in Ghana and thus not his coethnic. His friends are "both Ghanaians and Hausas." Indeed, his social network expands vastly beyond his Hausa brethren.

Sulaiman was jobless at the time of the 1969 Quit Order. His memory of it is stark, but his experience was quite different from Mary's. He neither witnessed nor endured harassment at the time. He made no effort to acquire a residence permit. Not only did he stay while thousands of Yorubas fled; all his friends – Ghanaians and Hausas – stayed as well.

The portraits presented in this section highlight two very different immigrant experiences in the same host country, Ghana. The Yoruba experience has been characterized by instability, fear, and exclusion. The Hausa experience, by contrast, has been almost trivial. This book sets out to explore and explain this divergence.

1.2 Three Assumptions Challenged

What explains immigrant exclusion in urban West Africa? Why do some immigrants display greater levels of attachment to their immigrant community than do others? Why do some immigrant

---

[3] Interview, Accra, Ghana: December 10(F), 2010. "Sulaiman" is a pseudonym used to protect the anonymity of the respondent.
[4] On March 28, 2007, the local magazine *Bilingual Free Press* ran an article in its *Hot Issues* section, entitled "Hausa: Is It a Ghanaian language?" (Sulley 2007).

groups seamlessly integrate into their host societies while others face exclusion and insecurity? Why do some countries expel their immigrants en masse while others never resort to this form of violence?

Scholars have long recognized the dynamic and political nature of citizenship in Africa and have demonstrated the various ways in which African leaders have manipulated citizenship for political gain. Until 1990, Cameroon's president Paul Biya – a southern Christian who rose to prominence under a northern Muslim president – emphasized national unity. But in the face of a threatening opposition, Biya played the sons-of-soil card and Balkanized his constituents along regional lines (Geschiere 2009; Konings 2001). In the Democratic Republic of the Congo, Mobutu manipulated the citizenship status of the Banyarwanda (or Banyamulenge) of South Kivu based on electoral competition and dynamics. And from the 1970s onward, Mobutu made it a habit of "affirming and then again denying Congolese citizenship for the Banyamulenge" (Geschiere 2009: 37; Manby 2009). In Nigeria, the riots pitting Hausa settlers against the indigenes of Plateau State revolved around access to, and exclusion from, state resources such as land, via the definition of indigeneity (Ostien 2009). In both South Africa and Botswana, black immigrant Africans or Makwerekwere – who oftentimes have lived in the country for decades – become scapegoats in times of economic hardship (Nyamnjoh 2006). In Zambia in the 1970s, the government launched a national registration campaign asking headmen to identify who among their villagers was a Zambian and who was not; in many instances, headmen "willingly vouched for Malawian and Rhodesian strangers who wanted to be accepted as Zambian citizens, thus avoiding their alien status" (Shack and Skinner 1979: 15).

In some cases, the fluidity of citizenship in the region has led to all-out civil war. In Côte d'Ivoire, the concept of *Ivoirité* has been used to characterize the country's southerners *only* and to exclude its northerners from access to increasingly scarce virgin forest-land for cocoa production (Woods 2003). This movement was born out of economic and political competition, specifically the 1995 and 2000 presidential elections, in which electoral rules were redefined to bar children of noncitizens from running for presidential office; these effectively shut out of the competition Alassane Ouattara, a Muslim northerner whose mother was allegedly born in Burkina Faso (Copnall 2007; Geschiere 2009; Manby 2009). By 2002, this source of contention devolved into the Ivoirian civil war, as Guillaume Soro, a Northerner, led a rebellion against President Gbagbo's government. Soro was quoted as saying: "Give us our identity cards and we hand over our Kalashnikovs" (Manby 2009: 11). Similarly, Sindou Cissé, a senior leader of the New Forces rebel group during the civil war, has explained why he does not hold Ivoirian identity papers: "Because my name is Sindou Cissé, and I sound like I come from Mali or Guinea, they would not give me an ID card. That is what we are fighting about" (Copnall 2007: 14).

Countless more examples illustrate how political entrepreneurs in Africa can and do manipulate the laws and concept of citizenship for instrumental gain.[5] Yet ever-increasing population flows both within and across African countries raise the challenge of incorporating, not only existing forms of ethnic and religious diversity, but new ones as well. In a region where political membership and exclusion are dynamic and fluid concepts, how are we to understand why some immigrant groups incorporate seamlessly into their host societies whereas others become easy scapegoats?

I argue that immigrant exclusion in urban West Africa is a function of the economic competition that characterizes relations between immigrant and indigenous traders, and of the bargains that immigrant community leaders strike with local police to become monopoly providers of immigrant security. Factors that facilitate individual immigrant assimilation threaten indigenous traders who compete with immigrants for access to scarce resources; they also jeopardize the positions of immigrant

---

[5] These examples also corroborate the claim in this book that while legislation on citizenship and immigration does exist in Africa (see Herbst 2000: chapter 8), it remains easily manipulable and manipulated on the ground.

community leaders who seek to protect their power and influence over a distinct group. As a result, cultural overlap between immigrants and hosts offers no advantage to immigrant integration and may, in fact, exacerbate immigrant exclusion.[6] When violence erupts, cultural overlap may lead to greater insecurity.[7]

In this book I develop and test this argument with a systematic comparison of two immigrant groups in three host cities. This work builds on the aforementioned literature on citizenship in Africa by focusing on the perspective of immigrant groups and host societies before the violence breaks out. In so doing, it offers micro-foundations for understanding immigrant exclusion in urban West Africa, and challenges three widely held assumptions about anti-immigrant politics.

Anti-Immigrant Politics Is also a South-South Issue

Academic scholarship and news media alike have focused overwhelmingly on South-to-North migration and on the problems immigrants face integrating into Europe, the United States, Canada, Australia, and New Zealand. This has conveyed the impression that immigration is a South-to-North phenomenon and that its politics revolve, naturally, around economic competition. The reasons for this emphasis on South-to-North migration are twofold. First, industrialized democracies are better equipped to record data about their immigrants. They have the state capacity to police their borders and register their migration flows. Second, major media sources are based out of these industrialized democracies and thus report on issues that are salient to them. South-to-North migration may have indeed been the

---

[6] The term "immigrant" is difficult to define and identify in the African context, where the concept of a sovereign nation is but a few decades old. Where citizenship status seldom protects against social or political violence, immigrant is less a legal depiction than an identity defined by ethnic origin. Here "immigrant" is used interchangeably with "nonindigenous ethnic group."

[7] The vocabulary used here assumes a key difference between "assimilation," which it uses to mean "the ability of a group to pass as another group," and "integration," which it uses to mean "the incorporation, or acceptance of the group, as it is."

predominant type of migration flow in the 20th century, and our focus on this phenomenon may have merely reflected reality; but because of lack of data on South-to-South migration, we may never know for sure.

This body of work views economic competition as one source of immigrant exclusion: immigrants from the developing world offer cheaper, more mobile labor and pose an economic threat to their hosts' labor force. The empirical work underlying this hypothesis is voluminous, yet inconclusive. Public opinion research has found that opposition to immigration increases during periods of economic recession (Burns and Gimpel 2000; Lapinski et al. 1997). Yet other studies yield more ambiguous results. In their analysis of the American National Economic Surveys (ANES) of 1992 and 1996, Burns and Gimpel found that individuals who expressed worse personal economic outlooks were more likely to *favor* increased immigration in 1992. Citrin, Green, Muste, and Wong found no significant relationship between personal economic assessments and attitudes toward immigration policy (Citrin et al. 1997).

One source of ambiguity in these aggregate trends in public opinion toward immigration is that host societies exclude some immigrant groups, but not others: not all immigrant groups pose a salient economic threat.[8] And it is economic competition among rival groups that produces hostile attitudes (Forbes 1997; Olzak 1992; Quillian 1995). Olzak, for example, analyzes the frequency and cause of ethnic conflict across major American cities between 1877 and 1914, at a time when immigration from Europe and Asia peaked. She finds that factors that raise competition between ethnic and racial groups, such as the desegregation of the labor market, also increase rates of collective action. She draws from Barth's early insight that two populations in overlapping niches will engage in competition and exclusion

---

[8] The literature on intergroup conflict informs us that groups tend to reject other groups when the latter pose a perceived threat to the former's relative position in society (Blumer 1958; Lieberson 1980; Quillian 1995; Sniderman et al. 2000).

(Barth 1969). The most recent work on immigration in industrialized democracies confirms that economic scarcity is a precondition to immigrant conflict in Europe (Dancygier 2010).[9]

The research in this book challenges the assumption that immigration and immigrant exclusion are a North-South phenomenon by focusing on South-to-South migration and analyzing the extent to which the economic-competition argument travels to the developing world. Today, we know that half of all international migrants settle in the developing world, including 10 percent in Africa. Contrary to popular belief, these are not refugees: in 2005, an estimated 17 million voluntary immigrants lived in Africa, compared to slightly more than 3 million refugees. And in some cases, these numbers are growing more rapidly than in Europe. Over the past twenty years, for example, West Africa has seen higher growth rates in its annual migrant stock than has Western Europe (see Figure 1.1).[10]

We hear about these migrants when violence breaks out, as it did in the townships of South Africa in the spring of 2008. Otherwise, South-to-South migration is a phenomenon that touches a sizable and growing community of people about which we know very little. When anti-immigrant violence does not erupt onto the front page of *The New York Times*, however, African countries are still hosts to increasingly diverse societies, posing both a challenge and an opportunity to the region. The opportunity lies in the economic potential that migrants bring; the challenge, in the economic competition they represent. In a region already struggling to develop economically and to integrate existing forms of racial and ethnic diversity, these issues are particularly salient.

---

[9] Dancygier (2010) offers a theory of immigrant conflict in Europe, where economic scarcity combined with immigrant electoral power yields immigrant-native conflict, whereas economic scarcity combined with immigrant electoral weakness yields immigrant-state conflict instead.

[10] Data on the number of refugees and international migrants is from the United Nations Department of Economic and Social Affairs, Population Division (2008). United Nations Global Migration Database (UNGMD). Available at: http://esa.un.org/unmigration/.

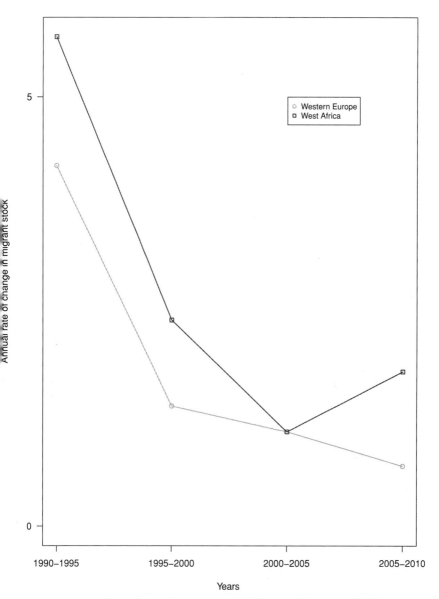

FIGURE 1.1. Growth in migrant stock in Western Europe and West Africa

South-South Anti-Immigrant Politics Defies the Clash of Civilizations

The alternative explanation for immigrant exclusion in industrialized democracies is a cultural one. This *clash of civilizations* argument identifies cultural difference as the culprit underlying immigrant exclusion.[11] The literature on social identity addresses this cultural-threat hypothesis. According to this theory, cultural, rather than economic, threats drive intergroup hostility. Individuals aim to evaluate the groups to which they belong positively, and this sometimes leads them to evaluate other groups negatively (Brewer 2001; Sniderman et al. 2004; Tajfel 1981; Tajfel and Turner 1979, 1986).[12] In this perspective, concerns about national identity drive immigrant exclusion because immigrants represent a threat to the hosts' national culture.

Public opinion surveys corroborate this hypothesis. Burns and Gimpel (2000) compare public opinions toward whites, Hispanics, and blacks and find that racial prejudice overwhelms economic concerns in predicting anti-immigrant attitudes. Lapinski and colleagues also consider divergent responses for different nationality groups. They find that, between the mid-1980s and the early 1990s, Americans held most favorable views toward Irish, Polish, Chinese, and Korean immigrants, followed by Vietnamese and Mexican immigrants, and finally by Iranian, Haitian, and Cuban immigrants (Lapinski et al. 1997: 2).

More recently, research that focuses on identifying the causal effect of cultural factors on immigrant exclusion further corroborates the cultural-threat explanation. In the Netherlands, Sniderman et al. (2004) use surveys with embedded experiments to assess the relative importance of economic versus cultural threats in determining individuals' attitudes toward immigrants. They find that concerns over national identity (cultural threats) determine exclusionary attitudes toward immigrants more than

---

[11] This term was famously used by Samuel Huntington in the context of post–Cold War global politics.

[12] In-group attachment or bias, however, does not necessarily lead to hostility toward out-groups (Allport 1954). Negative evaluations of out-groups is one strategy individuals use to ameliorate their in-group evaluation.

do concerns over economic interest (economic threats). Furthermore, they find that individuals are sensitive to what they call "situational triggers," or the priming of a certain identity: the priming of a Dutch national identity mobilizes support for immigrant exclusion beyond those already predisposed to perceive immigration as a threat (Sniderman et al. 2004: 45).

In Switzerland, where a number of municipalities have used referenda to vote on citizenship applications of foreign residents, country-of-origin stands out as the most important and significant predictor of citizenship attainment, eclipsing education level and employment status:

Rejection rates for applicants from former Yugoslavia and Turkey are about 40% higher compared to observably similar applicants from richer European countries.
(Hainmueller and Hangartner 2013: 159)

Cross-national analysis on anti-immigrant sentiment in Europe also substantiates a cultural argument over the conventional labor market competition hypothesis. Hainmueller and Hiscox (2007) analyze anti-immigrant sentiment across Europe using the 2003 European Social Survey and find that education and higher skills yield support for immigration regardless of immigrant skill level. Instead of finding that workers oppose immigrants with similar skill levels – an observable implication of the economic competition argument – they find that higher-educated individuals are more likely to value cultural diversity and to emphasize the net positive effect of immigration on the host economy. Anti-immigrant sentiment is thus a linear function of hosts' education level, because education places a higher premium on cultural diversity.

The hypothesis that cultural threats drive immigrant exclusion makes sense in industrialized democracies where national identities are well established and a large homogeneous majority exists. But how well does it travel to ethnically diverse places where national identities are only five decades old and citizenship is regularly redefined? The research in this book challenges the clash-of-civilizations argument by showing how cultural similarities between immigrant minority and host community offer no advantage for integration, and may even worsen immigrant exclusion and scapegoating. In this book I argue that immigrant group leaders face incentives to sharpen cultural boundaries in order to preserve the distinctive identity of the communities they lead. Furthermore, host society members feel threatened by, and are thus more likely to reject, immigrants who are culturally similar because their cultural repertoires offer them access to important and scarce resources. When it comes to immigrant exclusion in Africa, cultural similarities may become points of contention.

Resisting Assimilation Pays Off for Immigrants

Much of the literature on immigrant integration into industrialized economies tends to assume that assimilation into the host society is the end-goal for immigrants, and that it pays off. In-depth surveys of immigrant assimilation in the United States, for example, focus on factors that facilitate assimilation into a host society. The assumption is that immigrant groups strive to assimilate within set political, economic, and social frameworks in order to improve their socioeconomic opportunities (see, for example, Rumbaut and Portes 2001; Portes and Rumbaut 2001; Alba and Nee 2003). These immigrants may change the fabric of the host societies into which they integrate, but the dominant effect incontestably comes from the discrimination they face from their host government and labor market. The factors these authors identify leave little room for immigrant agency, and this makes sense in regions where the rules of the game are well defined and immigrants face a clear formal-legal path to citizenship.

Yet other scholars have focused on the incentives and strategies of minority groups to *resist* assimilation. By examining the benefits of marginality from a rational choice perspective, Laitin (1995) finds that certain groups derive economic benefits from their marginal status. Blalock (1967) and Bonacich (1973) have also demonstrated the advantages of middleman minority status. This literature accounts for the persistence of marginality among minorities such as Europe's Jews, the Indians of East Africa, the Lebanese of West Africa, and India's Untouchables.

This book shows that a similar phenomenon exists among immigrant groups in Africa, but for different reasons. Where states lack the capacity to monitor their borders and offer immigrants a formal-legal path to citizenship, immigrant communities tend to organize around informal leaders who become key actors in their integration process. These entrepreneurs offer immigrants – effectively their clients – protection and financial support, and they have an incentive to resist immigrant assimilation. When it comes to immigrant communities in Africa, resisting assimilation pays off.

This book elaborates this claim and challenges the aforementioned assumptions by introducing a systematic study of two migrant ethnic groups in three cities across West Africa, as well as a cross-national analysis of the determinants of immigrant expulsions across Africa. A first task is to expose the range of experiences South-to-South migrants face. This book does so on two levels. At the local level, I show that the same immigrant group may encounter benign neglect in one African city and open hostility in another. It may also organize effectively and visibly in one location and settle without much of a group identity in another. At the macro level, I expose how some leaders avidly scapegoat their immigrants while others do not. Between 1956 and 1999, more than 12 percent of African leader-terms and half of sub-Saharan African countries have expelled their immigrants en masse at least once. Yet while some countries, like the Democratic Republic of the Congo, expel their immigrants regularly, others, like Tanzania, never have.[13]

A second task is to offer an explanation for these divergent experiences. Scholarship on immigrant integration into industrialized democracies informs us that economic competition and cultural threats can aggravate immigrant exclusion. To what extent do these arguments explain immigrant exclusion in Africa?

---

[13] This is new information based on a dataset compiled by the author for this book. Chapter 5 elaborates on this source of data.

How might the insights we gain from research on South-to-North migration travel to African host societies? Do migrants always face a socioeconomic incentive to assimilate, and under what circumstances might they be better off resisting assimilation?

1.3 Overview of the Theory

In many African countries, the state lacks the capacity to police its own borders.[14] Consequently, host populations cannot rely on their state to successfully manage the flow of immigrants at various points of entry. Instead, immigrant policing occurs within the localities in which immigrants settle, through local-level bargains rather than national public policy. These processes require that we look at three different types of actors: the host societies in which immigrants settle, the leaders of immigrant communities, and the immigrants themselves.

Indigenous Hosts

Indigenous merchants compete with immigrant traders in the informal urban economy. In urban West Africa, where informal trading is a predominant form of economic activity, access to customers, loans, and supplies is typically achieved through cultural networks, such as ethnic or religious groups.[15] Furthermore,

---

[14] See Herbst (2000): chapter 8, for a discussion of the significance and porosity of African countries' national borders. Of course, some immigration in Africa follows a formal-legal path; this is typically the case for immigrants who migrate to attend a university and immigrants who are sent abroad by their employer. But the vast majority of immigration flows in Africa remains informal.

[15] In this book, culture refers to a set of shared symbols, a conceptualization used early on by Cohen (1969) to explain cultural change among Hausa migrants in Yorubaland. Laitin (1986) distinguishes this definition of culture from Geertz's conceptualization of culture as *webs of significance*. The former sees culture as a set of symbols that can be manipulated by political actors. The latter understands culture to comprise a system of "meanings embedded in shared symbols" (Laitin 1986: 16). In other words, Cohen's approach – and the approach in this book – is to focus on culture as a resource for collective action.

where the concept of citizenship remains fluid and ambiguous, cultural assimilation can protect an immigrant from police harassment and thus represents a critical sociopolitical resource. In sum, if the state cannot manage immigrant access to indigenous benefits, local actors in both host and immigrant communities take on a significant role, and an immigrant's shared cultural repertoire with her hosts becomes a defining criterion.

The implications of cultural similarity between immigrants and hosts – cultural overlap – are thus threatening to an indigenous merchant who wants to limit immigrant access to indigenous networks and benefits in the competition for scarce resources. For example, immigrants who share an ethnicity with members of their host society have the potential to use their ethnic networks to compete economically with their hosts. As a result, these immigrants benefit not only from the tight migrant networks that provide immigrants a comparative advantage in the economic realm (Greif 1993; Lalou et al. 1999), but also from their shared ethnicity with members of their host society, which provides security from police harassment and access to new indigenous business networks. Indigenous merchants thus face an incentive to monitor their ethnic borders to raise the cost of immigrant assimilation through cultural overlap and protect their indigenous benefits.[16] Consequently, high-overlap immigrants may face exclusion *because* of their shared cultural repertoires with their hosts.

Immigrant Leaders
The fate of most immigrants in West Africa depends largely on the informal bargains immigrant community leaders strike with local police to protect their constituents and preserve their own stature. Indeed, immigrant leaders are key actors with incentives to prevent individual immigrants from assimilating into their

---

[16] The argument that economic competition strains inter-ethnic relations, while economic complementarity promotes interethnic cooperation, has been made in other contexts (Jeon 2011; Jha 2007).

host society. Given these incentives, leaders engage in a set of strategies that raise barriers to immigrant assimilation, especially where the costs of passing as indigenous are low for the individual immigrant.

Leaders have a stake in preserving the distinct identity and organization of the groups they lead for two reasons. First, leaders gain financial and social benefits from their leadership positions (Sudarkasa 1979). Second, leaders face an altruistic incentive to sharpen ethnic boundaries in order to protect their constituents and promote interethnic cooperation (Fearon and Laitin 1996). Leaders work hard to protect their position: they succeed by offering conditional access to security and financial benefits to loyal constituents. They strike deals with local authorities that guarantee their group's protection, conditional on proof of membership and engagement in the immigrant community. Furthermore, leaders use pooled resources from membership dues and donations to provide financial support of various forms to loyal members. These include the repatriation of the deceased to the home country, start-up loans and credits for informal traders, and financial support for ceremonial gatherings such as weddings and funerals.

Shared cultural repertoires between immigrants and hosts pose a threat for immigrant leaders trying to preserve their status and the distinct identity of the groups they lead. Immigrants who share ethnic or religious traits with their hosts have an opportunity to access scarce resources through these cultural networks. Consequently, leaders of immigrant groups that share cultural overlap with their host society perceive a greater threat of defection on the part of their constituents, and seek to lock in these constituents by imposing institutional constraints on their access to the financial and security benefits they provide: high-overlap immigrants are required to display greater commitment to their immigrant community by participating in group activities, attending group meetings, or purchasing membership cards.

The outcome of immigrant leader strategies is that some immigrant groups are more formally organized and visibly mobilized than are others. In an effort to enforce loyalty, leaders of immigrant groups that overlap culturally with their host societies attempt to lock in their constituents' membership through formal organizations and institutions. Consequently, these immigrants display greater attachment to their immigrant community.

Immigrants

Individual immigrants are caught between the two dynamics described in the previous section. Immigrants may seek to reach out to their hosts to access new economic opportunities or achieve greater safety through social assimilation. In fact, research suggests that, all else being equal, combining dense in-group ties with key out-group ties is optimal for immigrant integration (Woolcock 1998). Yet fostering out-group ties remains an unlikely strategy for individual immigrants. Not only is it a risky move when hosts and immigrant leaders alike fear and seek to actively prevent immigrant assimilation; its opportunity cost may simply be too high: investing in immigrant networks rather than uncertain out-group ties provides the individual migrant with a social support system and a set of economic opportunities immediately upon arrival. In sum, individual immigrants face a *signaling imperative*, an incentive and a need to signal their commitment to their immigrant community in order to access group benefits and protection.

Summary

Cultural overlap represents significant opportunities to individual migrants seeking social and economic security in West Africa's host cities. But for that very reason, cultural overlap threatens immigrant-group leaders who seek to prevent member defection, group identity loss, and consequently the loss of their own stature. These leaders counter the threat of assimilation by striking bargains with local police that raise the cost of passing and in turn underscore the security benefits that leaders are able to provide. By locking in these new costs and benefits through formal institutions that both cement immigrant attachment to

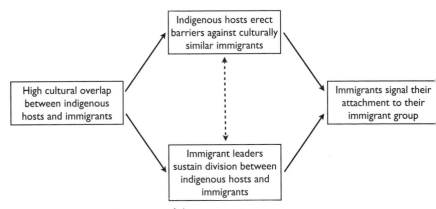

FIGURE 1.2. Summary of the argument

their immigrant community and offer immigrant security, leaders preserve their own roles. On the other side, cultural overlap generates an economic threat to indigenous merchants because economic competition in African urban centers relies heavily on the networks individuals can tap into for access to customers, loans, and supplies. Cultural traits thus become significant assets immigrants might use to their economic advantage, and as a result, a significant determinant of immigrant exclusion in Africa. Figure 1.2 summarizes the argument.

1.4 Scope

The argument in this book is counterintuitive: the claim that cultural similarities do not necessarily improve integration is a dissonant one to any researcher working on immigrant integration in industrialized countries. But in regions like West Africa, a different set of dynamics prevails. Horowitz (1985: 72) conveys this in his survey of ethnic conflict:

Whereas groups threatened with differentiation turn to the past to reduce their internal diversity, groups threatened with assimilation resort to their history to affirm their distinctiveness from those around them. Often begun by group members who are furthest along in the individual assimilation process, these movements commonly result in an explosive and violent assertion of group separateness.

Horowitz cites a number of examples, such as the Bakonjo of Western Uganda, the Kurds of Iraq, Syria, Iran, and Turkey, and the Sikhs in the Indian Punjab, who all went through a process of boundary reification in reaction to the possibility of assimilation. He argues that the threat of group identity loss has triggered cultural revivals that reify group boundaries, reducing individual cross-group mobility. Furthermore, Horowitz argues that intergroup hostility has accompanied this process of reification (Horowitz 1985: 72). This book builds on Horowitz's insights by showing when and how cultural similarity can become a threat. This section establishes three criteria that define the scope of the argument and thus highlight when cultural similarity is a source of affinity and when it becomes a point of contention.

First, the argument applies in countries where borders are porous and migrant communities cross over relatively indiscriminately. In many African countries, the state lacks the capacity to police its own borders. Herbst (2000: 253) has laid out this conventional wisdom about boundaries in Africa:

These boundaries are, as many have pointed out, arbitrary, porous, and sometimes do not have an immediate physical presence in the territories they are supposed to demarcate. Many people do cross the borders in search of opportunity, ranging from peasants who graze their cattle on both sides of the Zimbabwe/Mozambique border to professionals who migrate from Ouagadougou to Abidjan in search of a better job.[17]

Consequently, host populations cannot rely on their state to successfully manage the flow of immigrants at various points of entry. Instead, immigrant policing occurs within the localities in which immigrants settle, through local-level bargains rather than

---

[17] However, this does not mean that the state is absent. Indeed, as this book shows, state agents such as the police play a significant role in immigrant incorporation in urban West Africa. What is absent, therefore, is not state capacity altogether but rather a formalized, accountable method for incorporating migrants. Herbst (2000) captures this apparent contradiction well, with the claims that "Africa's territorial boundaries have enormous political significance, even if they do allow some people through.... Citizenship therefore had an immediate importance that should not be overlooked simply because the borders are weak" (Herbst 2000: 230–232).

national public policy. Because formal state obstacles barely exist to limit immigrant flows and access to scarce resources in their host countries, informal factors such as cultural repertoires (a shared language, or shared physical traits) become defining criteria for immigrant incorporation.

Second, the argument applies where the police act with relative impunity. In the absence of formal-legal venues for individual protection, local actors rely on personal relationships rather than impersonal institutions and policies for their security. Consequently, immigrant communities benefit from an immigrant entrepreneur who can strike deals with local authorities and deliver goods such as protection from civil and social harassment; similarly, host societies benefit from the existence and preservation of an easily identifiable and vulnerable minority that can attract police attention.

Third, the argument applies in urban centers with relatively undifferentiated economies, that is, in localities where the predominant economic activity is informal trading. In such settings, economic competition relies not on individual skill or education level, but rather on the networks individuals can tap into for access to customers, loans, and supplies. Using networks as economic assets is not a strategy unique to urban West Africa. Granovetter (1973, 1995) has demonstrated the significance of social networks in accessing jobs in the American context, for example. But scholars have shown that, where formal contract enforcement is unpredictable as in much of sub-Saharan Africa, social networks and personal trust underpin market transactions (Fafchamps 2004). Therefore, in urban West Africa, cultural traits become significant assets immigrants can use to their economic advantage. Consequently, cultural similarities may heighten, not alleviate, immigrant exclusion.

1.5 Empirical Strategy

Research Design

To measure and understand the roots of the variation in immigrant exclusion in Africa, I have followed two urban migrant

TABLE I.I. *Case Selection and Observable Implications*

Host City	Immigrant Group	Cultural Overlap	Host Society Exclusion	Immigrant Group Attachment
Accra	Hausa	Low: none	Low	Low
	Yoruba	High: religious	High	High
Cotonou	Hausa	Low: religious	Low	Low
	Yoruba	High: ethnic/religious	High	High
Niamey	Hausa	High: ethnic/religious	High	High
	Yoruba	Low: religious	Low	Low

trading communities in three West African cities over the course of twelve months of fieldwork in West Africa (see Figure 1.3). The Nigerian Yorubas and Hausas are similar on a number of parameters but differ in their ethnic and religious composition.[18] Accra (Ghana), Cotonou (Benin), and Niamey (Niger) are three West African urban centers that vary significantly in their ethno-religious makeup. The combination of immigrant group and host city accomplishes two methodological goals. First, it achieves a wide range of variation in the extent of cultural overlap between immigrants and hosts, from no cultural overlap (Hausas in Accra) to ethnic *and* religious overlap (Yorubas in Cotonou; Hausas in Niamey). Second, within each host city, this empirical strategy allows for comparisons between a relatively high-overlap group and a relatively low-overlap group; at the same time, the high-overlap group is not the same immigrant group across cities. Hence, this research design produces clear observable implications both across cities and between groups. The case selection and observable implications are summarized in Table 1.1.

Nigerian Hausas and Yorubas offer a strong basis for comparison because they share a country of origin, the British colonial

---

[18] This empirical strategy focuses on cultural traits that *can be shared* between immigrants and hosts, hence ethnicity and religion. Scholars have noted the political salience of hometown rather than religious identities among the Yoruba in Nigeria (Laitin 1986). However, hometown identities, by definition, cannot be shared between immigrants and hosts.

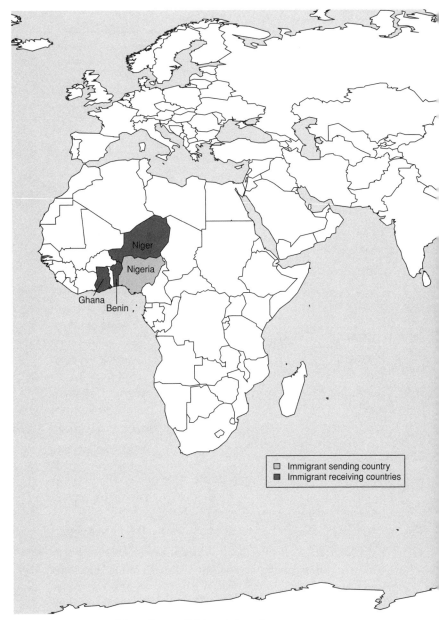

FIGURE 1.3. Map of 2007 fieldwork location

legacy, and a long-standing history of trade migration throughout West Africa. Indeed, both Nigerian Yorubas and Hausas have migrated from their homelands and throughout West Africa for more than a century (Igué 2003; Sudarkasa 1977). Hausas initially specialized in kola nut trade, while Yorubas originally sold traditional cloth. Both groups traveled by road to their final destinations with an economic intent to sell their goods abroad. Both settled in their host cities and have been living there for a century. In some localities, like Accra, both groups even fostered key ties with indigenous traditional authorities. The Yoruba, for example, built early connections with the Ga people of Accra, and many intermarried. Chief Brimah, the first Yoruba traditional leader to settle in Accra, was the first immigrant chief to be recognized by indigenous traditional leaders (Rouch 1956). Similarly, the Hausa became important authority figures in Accra's Zongo neighborhood, where Hausa eventually became the lingua franca for the city's Muslim community (Gomda 2006). By comparing Yoruba and Hausa migrant communities in Accra, Cotonou, and Niamey, this book compares groups that are similar in their timing, goal, and method of migration, but which vary in the cultural overlap they share with their host societies.

Data Collection

Explaining variation in immigrant exclusion in West Africa is an empirical challenge for a number of reasons. First, immigrant communities are *rare* populations, such that accessing these populations and gaining their trust was an important first step in the micro-level analysis of immigrant attitudes and behaviors. Second, systematic quantitative data on immigrant exclusion in West Africa do not exist. I thus had to devise measures of immigrant exclusion that captured both the immigrant and host perspectives. To do so, I developed survey instruments intent on capturing (1) immigrant attachment to a distinct immigrant community, through emotional, physical, financial, and institutional investment; and (2) host attitudes and behaviors of exclusion or inclusion vis-à-vis immigrants. I then spent approximately two months in each country, with the help of local research assistants, administering the surveys in some of the most densely populated and poorest areas of Accra, Cotonou, and Niamey. Working in tandem with young and dynamic enumerators who were themselves members of the immigrant communities I surveyed, I benefited from respondents' willingness to open up and to share their experiences as immigrants. Finally, in an effort to capture a richer, more comprehensive account of the immigrant experience in the region, I complemented the quantitative data collection with a more qualitative look into the lives of immigrants in Africa. I thus spent an additional one to two months in each city, meeting with immigrants and their community leaders to sketch out their experiences through semi-structured interviews. This effort benefited from the rapport I was able to establish early on with the leadership of the immigrant communities I studied. The field research in this book thus brings together multiple sources of data from West Africa in 2007 to build systematic and comprehensive measures of exclusion and attachment. In the sections that follow, I elaborate on this data collection process.

Surveys of Immigrant Communities: Hausas and Yorubas in Accra, Cotonou, and Niamey

The data collection process culminated into twelve months of work in West Africa to track the experiences of the Hausas and Yorubas of Accra, Cotonou, and Niamey. These immigrant populations are rare populations. And in West Africa, immigration flows are either not formally recorded or not publicly accessible.[19] The practical solution, therefore, is to obtain an availability sample of immigrants:[20] respondents are selected based

---

[19] Unsuccessful attempts were made to acquire data from the Immigration Office in Accra in January 2007.

[20] In Accra, an initial attempt was made to recruit immigrant respondents using a random-walk procedure in an area – Nima/Newtown – reputed to house numerous Nigerians and otherwise known as Lagostown. It took three hours to find the first Yoruba respondent. This method, which would have eventually yielded a random sample of Yoruba and Hausa immigrants, proved to be prohibitively costly and was abandoned.

on their availability rather than random sampling.[21] This creates obvious challenges for generalizability. But to ensure comparability, I recruited immigrant respondents from both ethnic groups in each of the three cities in systematically similar ways. In each city, I introduced myself and my project at the Nigerian High Commission. I was then given the names and contact information of ethnic community leaders from the three main Nigerian ethnic groups – the Igbo, Hausa, and Yoruba. Hausa and Yoruba leaders, along with other community entrepreneurs, were asked to identify young, dynamic, male community members who might be willing to work as my survey enumerators. I then spent approximately twenty to thirty days of work with my survey enumerator in each city, executing the survey.[22] I relied on my enumerator to identify the main Nigerian neighborhoods of Accra, Cotonou, and Niamey, respectively. Together we then approached respondents in these neighborhoods, described the project as an investigation into the lives of Yorubas and Hausas in Accra (Cotonou, Niamey), and recruited self-identified Nigerian Yorubas and Hausas. Each administered survey lasted approximately thirty to forty-five minutes, and we were able to complete ten surveys per day. A total sample size of 424 members of the Yoruba and Hausa immigrant communities in Accra (N = 184), Cotonou (N = 120), and Niamey (N = 120) was achieved.

Among other things, the survey instruments asked immigrants about the organizations to which they belong, the social networks they employed to acquire their job, the news media they follow, the frequency with which they travel to Nigeria, and the dimensions along which they identify. Furthermore, these surveys

---

[21] This is also the case in Internet click-in surveys. See Weisberg (2005) for a discussion. Statistical tests cannot be performed on a nonrandom sample. The analysis of immigrant survey data in Chapter 2 thus relies on sample comparisons, without tests of statistical significance.

[22] A pilot survey of N = 20 was first sent out in February 2007 in Accra; it was distributed to respondents for self-administration. The response rate was a mere 40%, and missing data was rampant. The decision was subsequently made to abandon self-administration and instead to administer the survey with a local community member as enumerator and translator.

TABLE 1.2. *Yorubas and Hausas in Accra and Niamey*

Host City	Immigrant Ethnic Group	
	Yoruba	Hausa
Accra	High overlap (religious)	Low overlap (none)
Niamey	Low overlap (religious)	High overlap (ethnic, religious)

collected data on a set of formal indicators of immigrant community attachment, by asking of which country respondents hold passports, whether they have a Nigerian Embassy identity card, where they vote in presidential elections, and whether they know the name of the president of their Nigerian community association. Each indicator was coded as a dichotomous variable, with "1" signifying attachment to the immigrant community and "0" otherwise. Averages were constructed from these sets of indicators, to yield an index of immigrant attachment in each city and for each immigrant group. Appendix 1 details the construction of the immigrant attachment index.

Surveys of Host Populations in Accra and Niamey

It takes two to integrate. In an effort to capture the flip side of immigrant exclusion and integration, I also collected data on host attitudes toward Yorubas and Hausas in Accra and Niamey. Recall, from the research design, that – relative to Hausas – Yorubas are high overlap in Accra but low overlap in Niamey. Table 1.2 illustrates the observable implication of the argument when it comes to the exclusion of Yorubas and Hausas in Accra versus Niamey: if shared cultural repertoires threaten hosts seeking to limit access to socioeconomic resources, then we expect Ghanaians to exclude Yorubas more than Hausas in Accra, but Nigeriens to exclude Hausas more than Yorubas in Niamey.

To test this observable implication, this book relies on original survey data collected on a random sample of indigenous residents of Accra (N = 200) and Niamey (N = 400) to measure host acceptance and rejection of Yorubas and Hausas. In each city, I recruited two local enumerators to execute a random-walk sampling methodology and administer a short questionnaire probing sentiments of political incorporation and exclusion of Yorubas and Hausas among the host populations. The city was divided into twenty equal, arbitrarily delineated but geographically contiguous areas. A landmark was arbitrarily chosen as the approximate center of each area. Each enumerator was assigned one landmark per half-day and instructed to return to the landmark after five random-walk iterations (e.g., after completing five questionnaires), so as to use the landmarks as a starting point twice, once for every five respondents. Random-walk instructions were generated via a random-number generator.[23] Twenty questionnaires were completed each day by each enumerator. The sampling method was designed to ensure that every area in the city had an equal probability of being covered. Figures 1.4 and 1.5 reproduce the maps and landmarks used in the execution of the random walk methodology in Accra and Niamey, respectively.

In Accra, the surveys were conducted in English or the respondent's preferred local language, and in Niamey, they were conducted in French or the respondent's preferred local language. Measures first developed by Posner (2004b) were used to gauge acceptance and rejection of immigrants, and an embedded experiment randomly assigned the type of questionnaire respondents received (the Hausa or the Yoruba questionnaire) in order to compare exclusionary attitudes. The two key questions used to measure exclusion were:

1. Do you think Ghanaians here would vote for a Hausa (Yoruba) if he were standing for President?
2. What about you: would you vote for a Hausa (Yoruba) if he were standing for President?

---

[23] These were then translated into instructions for the enumerator. For example, one set of random-walk instructions for recruiting one respondent reads, with emphasis on those factors determined via the random-walk generator: "Turn to your *right* and take *120* steps; approach the *5th woman* on your *left*."

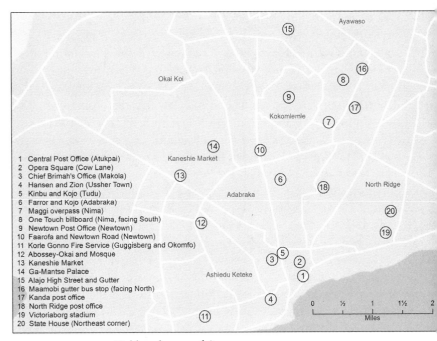

1 Central Post Office (Atukpai)
2 Opera Square (Cow Lane)
3 Chief Brimah's Office (Makola)
4 Hansen and Zion (Ussher Town)
5 Kinbu and Kojo (Tudu)
6 Farror and Kojo (Adabraka)
7 Maggi overpass (Nima)
8 One Touch billboard (Nima, facing South)
9 Newtown Post Office (Newtown)
10 Faarofa and Newtown Road (Newtown)
11 Korle Gonno Fire Service (Guggisberg and Okomfo)
12 Abossey-Okai and Mosque
13 Kaneshie Market
14 Ga-Mantse Palace
15 Alajo High Street and Gutter
16 Maamobi gutter bus stop (facing North)
17 Kanda post office
18 North Ridge post office
19 Victoriaborg stadium
20 State House (Northeast corner)

FIGURE 1.4. Fieldwork map of Accra

In Accra, 100 respondents were randomly asked about their attitudes of exclusion or acceptance toward Hausas, and the other 100 were randomly asked about their attitudes of exclusion or acceptance toward Yorubas. Neither immigrant group shares an ethnic overlap with the host society: there are no indigenous Yorubas or Hausas in Ghana. Half the Yoruba community, however, shares a Christian overlap with a largely Christian Accra. By contrast, the Hausa community is largely Muslim. Therefore, while both Yorubas and Hausas are nonindigenous ethnic groups in Accra, Yorubas are high-overlap immigrants relative to Hausas.

In Niamey, 100 respondents were asked about their attitudes of exclusion and acceptance toward Hausas; 100 respondents were asked about their attitudes of exclusion and acceptance toward Yorubas; 100 respondents were asked about their

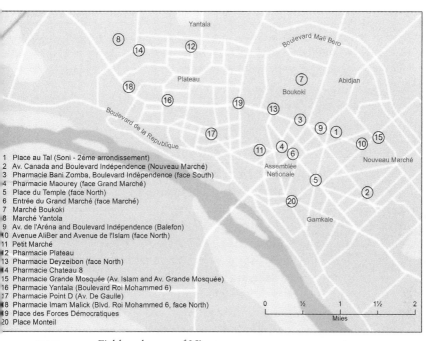

1 Place au Tal (Soni - 2éme arrondissement)
2 Av. Canada and Boulevard Indépendence (Nouveau Marché)
3 Pharmacie Bani Zomba, Boulevard Indépendence (face South)
4 Pharmacie Maourey (face Grand Marché)
5 Place du Temple (face North)
6 Entrée du Grand Marché (face Marché)
7 Marché Boukoki
8 Marché Yantola
9 Av. de l'Aréna and Boulevard Indépendence (Balefon)
10 Avenue AliBer and Avenue de l'Islam (face North)
11 Petit Marché
12 Pharmacie Plateau
13 Pharmacie Deyzeibon (face North)
14 Pharmacie Chateau 8
15 Pharmacie Grande Mosquée (Av. Islam and Av. Grande Mosquée)
16 Pharmacie Yantala (Boulevard Roi Mohammed 6)
17 Pharmacie Point D (Av. De Gaulle)
18 Pharmacie Imam Malick (Blvd. Roi Mohammed 6, face North)
19 Place des Forces Démocratiques
20 Place Monteil

FIGURE 1.5. Fieldwork map of Niamey

attitudes of exclusion and acceptance toward Kanawas; and 100 respondents were asked about their attitudes of exclusion and acceptance toward Katsinawas. I explain the introduction of these new ethnic group labels in the next paragraph.

In Niamey, Hausa immigrants share a significant ethnic overlap with the indigenous population. Indeed, approximately 55 percent of the population of Niger is Hausa (Central Intelligence Agency 2011b). This allows for an assessment of hosts' exclusionary attitudes toward immigrants who share with them an ethnic identity. Yet this also creates a problem in the wording of the acceptance and exclusion questions for Hausas. If the term *Hausa* in Niger does not connote *nonindigenous ethnicity* the way it does in Ghana, a respondent may interpret the question as one that asks about the acceptance and exclusion of indigenous Hausas. In fact, without any indication that the questions ask about *Nigerian* Hausas (a word that – if included in the survey instrument – would surely bias the respondent's answers unfairly toward exclusion, given that the term "Nigerian" was not used to describe Yorubas), we have no reason to believe that a Nigerien respondent would interpret the term Hausa as none other than a reference to the indigenous Hausas of Niger.

This problem is resolved with the addition of two more treatments, two new ethnic categories, the Kanawa and Katsinawa, in the Niger survey. These are subgroups of the Hausa ethnic group that refer to two of the historical Hausa city-states, Kano and Katsina, both in northern Nigeria. However, Katsinawas in Niger are generally considered to be an indigenous ethnic group while Kanawas are unambiguously indigenous to Nigeria.[24] Therefore, in order to measure Nigeriens' acceptance or exclusion of Hausas in a place where indigenous Hausas abound, the key term used is "Kanawa," an ethnic group whose indigenous origins are unambiguously outside Niger (just like the Yoruba), yet one that is Hausa nonetheless. To summarize, the relevant questionnaires used in the Niamey sample were questionnaires on Yorubas (N = 100) and Kanawas (N = 100).[25] Both are nonindigenous to Niamey. Kanawas, who share an ethnicity and a religion with Niamey hosts, are higher-overlap immigrants than their Yoruba counterparts, who share merely a religion – Islam – with Niamey society.

[24] Extensive conversations with survey enumerators were instrumental in devising this solution. When the Fulani jihad leader Usman dan Fodio conquered Katsina in 1804, Katsina's Hausa nobility resettled and proclaimed a Hausa Katsina chiefdom in Maradi (in modern-day Niger). This explains why Katsinawas are not unambiguously indigenous to Nigeria. Kanawas, on the other hand, are.

[25] Hausa (N = 100) and Katsinawa (N = 100) questionnaires were used as well in order to verify that the data corroborated the intuition. They do: exclusion rates for Hausas are approximately 5–6%, and exclusion rates for Katsinawas are approximately 20–25%, much lower than exclusion rates for Yorubas and Kanawas. This is consistent with the fact that Hausa and Katsinawa are not nonindigenous ethnic groups while Yoruba and Kanawa are nonindigenous ethnic groups in Niger.

It is important to reiterate the identification strategy for measuring host exclusion of Hausas and Yorubas in Accra and Niamey. Questions of political incorporation were used in conjunction with nonindigenous ethnic markers to capture exclusion. In Accra, the two nonindigenous ethnic markers were *Yoruba* and *Hausa*. In Niamey, they were *Yoruba* and *Kanawa*. In each case, the two labels are equally nonindigenous ethnic markers. Differential responses of hosts' willingness to vote for one or the other presidential candidate should thus give us an idea of how politically incorporated these groups are: these questions are meant to measure the extent to which indigenous hosts can conceive of a Hausa or a Yoruba as a member of his or her polity. Debriefing sessions with the survey enumerators in Accra confirm that these questions captured this process quite well. In thinking about the voting questions, respondents wondered out loud precisely whether or not the Hausa/Yoruba was Ghanaian. Those who answered "no" most often justified it with the claim "They're not Ghanaians!" and those who answered yes claimed instead that "They are Ghanaians, so if they present themselves as candidates, and they are good, I should vote for them."[26]

Interviews with Victims of Ghana's 1969 Alien Compliance Order in Ogbomosho, Nigeria

The data collection process relies predominantly on attitudinal measures of immigrant attachment and exclusion (respondents' beliefs, opinions, attitudes). In an effort to incorporate behavioral outcomes as well, I included a brief study of the effects of Ghana's 1969 Alien Compliance Order – a mass immigrant expulsion that affected more than 100,000 aliens (Sudarkasa 1979).[27] The goal was to identify, in a moment of sociopolitical violence and chaos, which immigrant groups were targeted. In May 2007, I traveled to Ogbomosho, Nigeria, with a Christian Yoruba research assistant I had met during my fieldwork

---

[26] Debriefing session with Accra survey enumerators in Accra: April 30, 2007.

[27] Some claim this expulsion affected upward of 500,000 aliens (Adepoju 1984; Sise 1975).

in Accra. Ogbomosho is a major emigrant town that has sent waves of Yoruba economic migrants to Ghana since the early twentieth century. Using a snowball sampling methodology, we interviewed forty-three Yorubas who had been in Ghana at the time of the Compliance Order of 1969. Note that these respondents were not easy to find. The expulsion occurred in 1969, meaning that many of its victims have since passed away. We relied on the Ogbomosho Christian Baptist network, of which my research assistant was a member, to track down some of the remaining survivors of this expulsion. Our first few participants provided other names, and so on. This recruiting method, while useful in seeking out members of a significantly rare population, poses important limits on generalizability. For example, over the course of four weeks, forty Christian Yorubas and only three Muslim Yorubas were interviewed, a bias attributable to the fact that my enumerator was himself a Christian Yoruba and that Ogbomosho is today a largely Christian town.[28] Still, the data collected provide important information on the expulsion experience, as we gathered data from a disappearing community and provided insight into which immigrants are targeted and which are spared when violence breaks out.

Interviews with Community Members and Leaders in Accra, Cotonou, and Niamey

Finally, qualitative interviews with more than 100 Hausas and Yorubas provide a richer understanding of immigrant experiences in host societies. Throughout 2007, following the same snowball sampling methodology I used for my surveys, I regularly interviewed immigrant community leaders and immigrants in Accra, Cotonou, and Niamey. Notably, all community leaders of the Hausa and Yoruba groups in all three cities were interviewed, using the same systematic method: the names of ethnic community leaders were provided by the Nigerian High Commission; I introduced myself to these leaders as a scholar studying the

---

[28] A parallel set of interviews in Ilorin, Nigeria, would balance out the ratio of Muslim to Christian Yorubas.

Yorubas and Hausas in Accra (Cotonou, Niamey); and I administered a semi-structured interview aimed at capturing leaders' incentives vis-à-vis their constituents, and the strategies they use to meet such incentives. The interview process was thus systematic across host localities.

Summary of Empirical Findings

The data indicate that leaders of high-overlap immigrant groups are acutely aware of the opportunities their members have to exploit shared cultural repertoires to access scarce resources from their host societies. Furthermore, the data confirm that high-overlap immigrants are – counterintuitively – more likely to demonstrate attachment to their immigrant community. Finally, the data show that indigenous members of host societies consistently exclude high-overlap groups more than they do low-overlap groups. In Christian Accra, Christian Yorubas share religious similarities with Ghanaians while Hausas, who are overwhelmingly Muslim, are culturally distinct. Yet survey and interview data indicate not only that Hausas are significantly less excluded than their Yoruba counterparts, but also that Muslim Yorubas are significantly less excluded than Christian Yorubas. In Niamey, Nigerian Hausas share a wide cultural repertoire with indigenous Nigeriens through both a shared ethnicity (Hausa) and a shared religion (Muslim). Yet survey and interview data indicate that these migrants are more excluded in Niamey than are their Yoruba counterparts.

1.6 Implications of the Research

The findings in this book challenge the conventional wisdom we have accumulated about immigrant exclusion over decades of studying immigrants in industrialized democracies. Furthermore, they carry important implications for human rights, development, and identity in Africa.

The challenge of immigrant inclusion and integration in Africa is a basic human rights issue that the international community has ignored. Between 1956 and 1999, 51 percent of sub-Saharan

African countries expelled their immigrants en masse, affecting a median 8,500 immigrants each time.[29] Most African immigrants in Africa live precarious lives, fearing deportation and extortion. Their vulnerability lies, in part, in the absence of a formal, institutionalized system of immigrant incorporation. Immigrant communities thus live at the mercy of local actors who share an incentive to preserve and exploit this vulnerability.

And yet, the successful integration of immigrant communities may create healthy economic competition that can spur growth in host societies; immigrant exclusion thus implies opportunity costs for African host countries. Scholars have shown that immigrant communities contribute to the expansion of trade networks and capital flows within and between countries. Yoruba migrants, for example, developed commerce and the Esusu institution of rotating credit throughout West Africa (Igué 2003). Hausa migrants expanded the kola nut and cattle trade from northern to southern Nigeria (Cohen 1969). Lebanese and Fula merchants developed commercial trade between Freetown and the Protectorate in Sierra Leone (Jalloh 1999). Maghrebi traders instituted long-distance trade across North Africa (Greif 1993). Such immigrant trading communities create new resources by expanding trade and capital flows. Host countries bent on limiting economic competition from groups that are highly motivated to invest and work suffer a cost.

This book further highlights the role that identity networks, rather than education and skills, play for immigrant integration in many developing countries (Cornelius et al. 2002): these networks determine the kinds of economic opportunities individuals can access. Immigrant traders rely on their ethnic and religious networks for social and economic support in their host localities. Furthermore, they depend on their immigrant community leaders for their own safety in places where the police act with impunity. Cultural networks thus constitute a critical economic

---

[29] The median, rather than the mean, is reported here as a measure of central tendency because a handful of expulsions targeted a very large number of immigrants. The mean is thus skewed to more than 138,500 immigrants.

and social resource that individuals use for protection and personal benefit. Imposing conditions for access to network benefits and adopting exclusionary attitudes to raise barriers to entry into a network are strategies that actors use when they compete for scarce resources (Fearon 1999).

Additionally, the research in this book suggests that African borders, while arbitrary, significantly shape group relations and identity. Borders have the potential to sour relations between coethnics across national boundaries. Miles and Rochefort (1991) previously made this point when they found that Hausas in Nigeria and in Niger feel closer to their non-Hausa conationals than they do to their coethnics across the border. Similarly, the findings in this book suggest that ethnic overlap between immigrants and hosts does not necessarily facilitate immigrant integration; it may, in fact, limit it. The national border that separates coethnics may be arbitrary; it is not insignificant.

Finally, the findings in this book highlight the institutional origins of ethnic identity and relations by focusing on the incentives actors have to sharpen group boundaries. Conventional wisdom tends to assume that cultural proximity improves group relations. Gradstein and Schiff (2006) argue that the social cost of minority integration into a majority depends, among other factors, on the cultural distance between the two groups. Sniderman et al. (2004) claim that the prominence of group differences, such as skin color, manner of dress, and language, increases the salience of concerns over national identity on the part of the host country. Posner (2004b) compares the Chewas and Tumbukas in Malawi and the Chewas and Tumbukas in Zambia in order to "rule out the possibility that the difference in the salience of the Chewa-Tumbuka cleavage was a product of greater objective differences between these groups on one side of the border than on the other" (Posner 2004b: 533).

In these perspectives, the less alike A and B are, the less likely A and B will integrate; conversely, the more alike A and B are, the more likely A and B will integrate. This assumption, however, overlooks the fact that cultural entrepreneurs in both minority and majority groups face incentives to highlight differences and reify boundaries (Barth 1969; Brass 1997; Fearon 1999; Fearon and Laitin 1996; Laitin 1995, 1998; Wilkinson 2006). Consistent with this approach, this book argues and finds that in certain contexts, the more alike A and B are, the more susceptible A and B become to boundary creation: the responses of key actors to cultural similarities between A and B may overwhelm the direct effect of cultural affinity in determining group relations. Which two groups are alike or not is no longer an objective reality.

1.7 Plan of the Book

The rest of this book is organized in the following manner. After this introduction, Chapter 2 asks why immigrant groups display varying levels of attachment to their immigrant communities in the societies that host them. It considers how, in the same host society, one immigrant community organizes into a tight, formal association, on which its members rely for access to social and financial resources, while another maintains a looser, informal network whose members do not necessarily exploit for socio-economic support. This chapter shows specifically how and why immigrants who share cultural traits with indigenous members of their host societies are more likely to signal their attachment to their immigrant group than do immigrants who do not share cultural characteristics with indigenous members of their host societies. It explains this outcome as the result of incentives that immigrant leaders face to sharpen cultural boundaries in order to preserve the distinctive identity of the communities they lead, and of the incentives individual immigrants face to signal their membership and commitment to their immigrant community in order to access the benefits they offer. The greater the cultural similarities between immigrants and hosts, the greater the signaling imperative and the tighter the immigrant association. The chapter tests the observable implications of this argument using interview and survey data collected among the Yoruba and Hausa immigrant communities of Accra, Cotonou, and Niamey, and shows that immigrant community attachment is greater where cultural overlap between immigrants and hosts is higher. The findings in this chapter suggest that the ethno-religious land-scapes into which immigrant communities settle carry significant consequences for the degree of attachment immigrants retain with their immigrant communities.

Chapter 3 then turns to the hosts. It argues and shows that immigrant groups who share cultural traits with their host societies may be more likely to experience greater exclusion from their hosts. This is so because indigenous merchants are directly threatened by the implications of cultural overlap and increase their hostility toward groups who they perceive can more easily assimilate through the cultural networks they share with their host societies. This chapter draws from surveys with embedded experiments from host societies in Accra and Niamey to demonstrate that high-overlap groups face greater exclusion than do low-overlap groups. Together, Chapters 2 and 3 provide empirical evidence that cultural differences may be endogenous to actors' strategies for highlighting cultural boundaries.

Chapter 4 offers a more in-depth analysis of alternative accounts, and shows that cultural overlap best explains patterns of immigrant exclusion for the cases in this book. Namely, this chapter considers a number of robustness checks for the empirical tests introduced in Chapter 3; it considers whether geography can better explain patterns of immigrant integration and exclusion, or whether certain types of immigrants select into certain types of host societies. Finally, it addresses questions of survey validity. This chapter thus offers additional pieces of evidence that corroborate the argument in this book.

Chapter 5 departs from the micro-level analysis of immigrant exclusion in West Africa and uses a cross-national statistical analysis to understand the determinants of mass immigrant expulsions. Expulsions are costly for both those expelled and those doing the expelling. Why, then, do some African leaders expel their immigrants while others do not? This chapter uses statistical analysis of an original dataset of mass immigrant expulsions in Africa to identify larger patterns of immigrant exclusion and violence. The analysis suggests that mass expulsions are significantly correlated with a country's economic and ethnic landscape. This chapter thus elucidates, on a larger scale, when and why African leaders choose to scapegoat their immigrants.

In the conclusion, Chapter 6 contextualizes this book's findings within the literature on immigrant exclusion, suggesting that the debate between economic and cultural determinants of exclusion may, for urban West Africa at least, create a false dichotomy. The chapter then opens up the discussion to further questions, calling for a richer research agenda that systematically incorporates the other half of all international migration flows: South-to-South migration.

2

Immigrants and Their Leaders

Karim is a Nigerian Hausa who traveled from his hometown in Kano (Nigeria) to Accra (Ghana) eight years ago to seek, among other things, a better livelihood. He arrived without a job or resources and had to rely on the kindness of a fellow Nigerian Hausa he met arriving in Accra, who housed and supported him financially for a week. He found his first job through a walk-in interview at a health service company that had advertised the opening on a billboard. He found his second job through a connection he made with his first employer. His wife and children live with him in a suburb of Accra. He is fluent in his native Hausa, in English, and in Twi, the most widely spoken Ghanaian language. He is currently learning Ga, the indigenous language of Accra. On weekends, he joins other Hausas to study the Koran. When he first arrived in Ghana, he did not seek the help or assistance of the Hausa community organization: he did not even know it existed. He eventually found out that it did through a friend but, he claims, "compared to the Yorubas and the Igbos, they don't do as much."[1]

---

[1] Interview, Accra, January 29(B), 2007. "Karim" is a pseudonym used to protect the anonymity of the respondent. The Igbo are an ethnic group indigenous to southeastern Nigeria.

Michael is a Nigerian Yoruba who traveled from his hometown in Ogbomosho (Nigeria) to Accra (Ghana) in 1989. He arrived as a trader transporting and selling goods between Nigeria and Ghana. His sister and uncle, who were already settled and working in Accra, loaned him money and offered him a place to stay to assist him upon arrival. Because of financial difficulties and a stroke of bad luck, he is currently unemployed. He spends his time at the Mark Hayford Memorial Baptist Church in downtown Accra, a large and lively church whose membership is largely Yoruba. He finds support from family and friends in the church. His wife, a Yoruba who was born in Ghana and whom he met through the church in Accra, is back in Nigeria with their three children. He speaks Yoruba and English fluently. He speaks only a little bit of Twi. He is an active member of the Yoruba Community and of his hometown association, the Ogbomosho Parapo, where Yorubas "help each other out, especially if people get in trouble."[2]

This chapter asks why immigrants display varying levels of attachment to their immigrant communities in the societies that host them. In the same host society, one immigrant community organizes into a tight, formal association on which its members rely for access to social and financial resources; meanwhile, the other maintains a looser, informal network whose members do not necessarily tap into for socioeconomic support. This chapter shows specifically how and why immigrants who share cultural traits with the indigenous members of their host societies end up signaling greater attachment to their immigrant group than do immigrants who do not share those cultural characteristics. It explains this outcome as the result of incentives that immigrant leaders face to sharpen cultural boundaries in order to preserve the distinctive identity of the communities they lead, and of the incentives individual immigrants face to signal their membership and commitment to their immigrant community in order to access the benefits they offer. I call this the immigrant's signaling

---

[2] Interview, Accra, January 29(A), 2007. "Michael" is a pseudonym used to protect the anonymity of the respondent.

imperative and argue that it can increase with cultural overlap between immigrants and hosts. I test the argument using interview and survey data collected among the Yoruba and Hausa immigrant communities of Accra, Cotonou, and Niamey, and show that immigrant community attachment is greater where cultural overlap between immigrants and hosts is higher.

I begin with an explanation of the incentives individual immigrants and their leaders face in their host societies. I then highlight the threat that cultural overlap represents and catalog the various strategies leaders have devised to deal with this threat. Next I turn to the data. I first present qualitative evidence substantiating the perspective of the immigrant leader. Then I analyze survey evidence of Yoruba and Hausa immigrant attachment in Accra, Cotonou, and Niamey. Additionally, I consider in greater detail the case of the Yorubas in Accra, who are divided along religious lines, and test the argument's observable implications on the attachment levels of Christian and Muslim Yorubas in a largely Christian Accra. Finally, I turn to qualitative interviews with Yoruba immigrants in Ghana to explore empirically the incentives they might have to resist assimilation.

2.1 Immigrant Options in Host Societies

Individual immigrants face a choice upon entering their host society: a migrant can seek socioeconomic opportunity by either reaching out to host society members (fostering out-group ties) or turning to one's own immigrant community members (relying on in-group ties). Some may do both.[3] Yet the benefits that immigrant community networks bring to the individual migrant are tangible. Not only do they provide a social support system upon arrival; they offer a venue of economic opportunity for a migrant in search of work. A new Yoruba migrant in Accra, for example, can obtain a loan to start her business when she attends meetings for her hometown association. Even if immigrants are

---

[3] Research, in fact, suggests that immigrants *should* do both to optimize access to new and existing resources (Woolcock 1998).

better off in the long run coordinating to invest in out-group ties because these might open up new economic opportunities or ensure greater safety through social assimilation, this choice is a risky one for any individual immigrant.[4] Instead, these immigrants face an incentive to signal their commitment to their immigrant community in order to access key benefits, such as money and safety.

Yet immigrants who share cultural traits with their host societies have opportunities to join indigenous networks and diversify their resources. For example, a Christian immigrant in Accra can join one of many Christian churches, attend a worship service he is familiar with, and make new business contacts through a common religious institution and identity. Similarly, a Nigerian Hausa can set up shop in Niamey and conduct business with Nigeriens without having to learn a new indigenous language because Hausa is already an indigenous language of Niger.

Individual immigrant defection from the immigrant group is unlikely. Even so, when immigrants share cultural traits with their host society, the ease of fostering out-group ties and the threat of immigrant defection increase, at least in the eyes of the immigrant community leader.

2.2 Immigrant Leaders and the Threat of Cultural Overlap

The immigrant community leader is a critical and ubiquitous element to the urban West African immigrant experience, one that shapes the way immigrant communities integrate into societies that lack formal-legal channels of immigrant incorporation. Immigrant leaders are well-known members of their community who are either elected or nominated to their leadership position. The Yoruba leaders in Accra and in Cotonou are elected Chairmen of the Yoruba Association; the Yoruba leader in Niamey is the Yoruba Chief, a hereditary position. Each leader is

---

[4] Scholars formalize the process as a tipping point: see Schelling (1978), Laitin (1994), Laitin (1998).

surrounded by an executive council of elected and nominated members.

Leaders accrue financial and social benefits by virtue of their position. Leadership councils collect regular contributions from their members, both in the form of annual dues and in the form of charitable donations at meetings and events. Leaders oversee the disbursement of these funds. They also enjoy social status and recognition, both on the part of their immigrant constituents and on the part of local officials in their host society. They become popular and socially influential members of their community by virtue of the very authority they herald.

Leaders have a stake in preserving the distinct identity and organization of the groups they lead for two reasons. First, leaders gain financial benefits and social benefits from their leadership positions.[5] A distinctive group organization thus constitutes the very basis for the benefits they reap, such that leaders want to prevent immigrant assimilation. Second, leaders face an altruistic incentive to sharpen ethnic boundaries in order to protect their constituents and promote interethnic cooperation. Indeed, interethnic cooperation arises, in part, because individual group members choose not to retaliate against an aggression by members of another group when they expect group leaders to police their own constituents (Fearon and Laitin 1996). This mechanism provides ethnic group leaders with an incentive to sharpen boundaries in order to promote cooperation between ethnic groups.[6] The same applies for immigrant group leaders who strike bargains with the police in their host communities to gain the authority they need to monitor and protect their constituents.

---

[5] Sudarkasa (1979), in her account of stranger communities in Kumasi, Ghana, from 1900 onward, provides a useful exposition of the benefits that accompany the position of immigrant community leader, and the conflicts such benefits created in the city's Zongo quarters.

[6] Fearon and Laitin reach the same conclusion by saying that "there is a rationale and interest for leaders of ethnic groups to limit interactions between coethnics and other groups, that is, to construct boundaries" (Fearon and Laitin 1996: 731).

Leaders who want to preserve their own social and financial benefits as well as the in-group policing mechanism that keeps their members safe are keenly aware of the opportunities individual migrants face to access indigenous networks. These opportunities threaten leaders' positions as monopoly suppliers of immigrant protection. When overlapping traits lower the risks – real and perceived – of fostering out-group ties, leaders counter the threat of immigrant defection by imposing greater signaling conditions on immigrant access to group benefits,[7] and individual immigrants have little choice but to comply in order to build the social capital necessary to access these critical resources.

In sum, when cultural overlap raises the threat of individual immigrant defection, the signaling imperative increases for individual migrants. Leaders are able to impose stricter signaling conditions because they control the group benefits immigrants seek: (1) protection from social and civil harassment and (2) financial support. Immigrants are willing to comply because their leaders' strategies amplify the costs of individual defection.

How do leaders successfully increase the signaling imperative for individual immigrants? To protect their constituents, immigrant leaders strike deals with local state officials that guarantee their group's protection conditional on proof of engagement in the immigrant community. Leaders act as guarantors of their members' security, using their own connections with the local police to protect and bail out their loyal constituents. Immigrants enjoy their leaders' protection as long as they demonstrate their active participation in, and commitment to, their immigrant community. Sudarkasa (1979) has documented how, through town unions, Yorubas were able to maintain community cohesion and organization in Ghana. In a survey of Yoruba communities in Kumasi, Sudarkasa explains how the creation of the Yoruba town union, or *Parapo*, during the late 1920s and 1930s, aimed at

---

[7] This argument does not presuppose that immigrants cannot both foster out-group ties and maintain in-group ties. Instead, this argument relies on the fact that leaders perceive the opportunity to foster out-group ties as a threat to the maintenance of in-group ties. Leaders react based on that perception.

maintaining and promoting group cohesion among the growing Yoruba community in Ghana: "Between the 1940s and 1960s, the Yoruba developed a network of associations known as Parapos (Unions), which were designed to promote solidarity and maintain order within the Yoruba community, and to facilitate the articulation of that community with the colonial government, the Ashanti host community, and the other ethnic communities with which the Yorubas had contact in Kumasi" (Sudarkasa 1979: 153). Parapos played two important roles for the Yoruba. First, they protected the community's good name through self-policing and self-adjudicating mechanisms. Second, they enabled Yoruba migrants to avoid paying the dues and fees that came with the use of formal institutions of justice and order in the larger Ghanaian society: "On various occasions different Parapos in Kumasi had sent delegations to the police station to plead for the release into their custody of a member who had been arrested for a minor offense, such as fighting in the market" (Sudarkasa 1979: 155). In fact, the Parapo actively dissuaded members from using Ghanaian courts by imposing fines against those who bypassed the Parapo authority, the most serious sanction being the repatriation of the offender to Nigeria. Compliance with Parapo rules was obtained through peer pressure from relatives and friends, along with Parapo officials: "The decisions of the Parapo councils (comprised of the officers and most highly respected elders) were usually adhered to because normally a Yoruba would not want to incur the consequences of alienating the Parapo elders and, more especially, of alienating his family and friends" (Sudarkasa 1979: 154).

Today the Parapo continues to maintain community cohesion and organization for immigrant Yorubas. But another institutionalized form of community cohesion and organization has taken hold for Nigerians in West Africa: the Embassy identity card, a formal document that is recognized by local authorities and protects immigrants from arbitrary harassment. Obtaining the card for his members is one of the main functions of the immigrant community leader: leaders facilitate access to this card for their loyal members and enforce preconditions for such access.

Regular renewal of the card – every year in some localities, every two years in others – prevents immigrants from defecting once they acquire it.

Why do local authorities strike deals with immigrant leaders? First, such arrangements guarantee a flow of money for the police, who can collect funds more steadily from reliable and resourceful immigrant community leaders rather than haphazardly from individuals who may or may not have resources. Second, such arrangements guarantee cooperation on the part of immigrant community leaders, who – through the access they have to their constituents – can help the police exert better and more efficient control over immigrants. The police benefit, therefore, from the in-group policing immigrant leaders offer.

A second strategy leaders use to secure their monopoly position and limit constituent defection is the control over members' access to monetary funds. Leaders use pooled resources from membership dues and donations to provide financial support of various forms: the repatriation of the deceased to the home country, start-up loans and credits for informal traders; and financial support for ceremonial gatherings such as weddings and funerals. For example, the Public Relations Officer of the Organization of Nigerian Citizens in Niger grew from a young apprentice tailor working for his mentor when he first arrived in Niamey a decade ago to a self-employed tailor who lives and runs his tailoring shop in the office space held by the organization. He enjoys rent-free living and working space; furthermore, many of his clients are staff members of the Nigerian Embassy in Niamey, clients he acquired through his connections with the leadership of the Nigerian community union. From his perspective, the economic benefits he accrued over time were directly correlated with his participation in the Nigerian community union.[8] The financial benefits that come with engagement in the immigrant association, and over which immigrant community leaders maintain control, are evidently far from trivial.

---

[8] Interview by the author with the Public Relations Office for the Nigerian Community Union in Niamey, Niger: March 2, 2007.

The Yoruba Parapo and the Embassy identity cards are two examples of institutionalized mechanisms for community cohesion and organization. They play a key role when cultural overlap between immigrants and hosts threatens an immigrant leader's position as a monopoly supplier of financial and civil security for immigrants. An immigrant who can tap into indigenous cultural networks for socioeconomic opportunity does not need her leader's services as much as an immigrant with no alternative source of support. Immigrant leaders of high-overlap groups thus counter the threat they perceive of immigrant defection by imposing greater signaling conditions on individual migrants. They offer full access to group benefits to those who have built sufficient social capital by actively participating in group activities and investing in group ties and institutions. They enforce these conditions more or less strictly depending on the severity of the threat of immigrant defection, that is, depending on the level of cultural overlap shared between immigrants and hosts.

Individual immigrants abide by these signaling conditions because they need to access immigrant group benefits. The costs of losing access to the financial and civil protection that immigrant leaders offer are so high in localities lacking formal-legal rights and individual protections that individual migrants face a strong incentive to comply with the conditions leaders impose. Hence, individual migrants trying to foster social capital with their leaders will signal their group commitment formally, by purchasing formal membership, and informally, by investing in social and institutional ties with their immigrant community.

In sum, leaders offer two types of club goods to their members: a minimum level of social and civil security, and access to financial resources. When cultural overlap between immigrants and hosts is high, the signaling imperative increases. Leaders induce immigrant attachment to their community by setting and enforcing conditions on members' access to these resources. Individual immigrants comply to assuage their leaders' fears and obtain the social capital they need to enjoy group benefits. In other words, high-overlap immigrants who wish to access the club goods leaders offer will signal their commitment to their immigrant group, both formally – by becoming formal members and buying into the formal organization of the group – and informally, through their every day commitment to their immigrant community.

2.3 Empirical Tests of Cultural Overlap and Immigrant Attachment

What the Immigrant Leaders Say

This chapter argues that leaders of immigrant communities aim to prevent immigrant assimilation into their host society, and do so through the exclusive benefits they offer selectively to loyal members. When we examine what the immigrant leaders say, we seek to determine whether leaders care about immigrant defection and what they do to prevent it. Interviews with immigrant community leaders in the Hausa and Yoruba communities of Accra, Cotonou, and Niamey and with local police in Cotonou confirm three aspects of the argument. First, immigrant leaders are keenly aware of the opportunities their constituents have to defect, especially where cultural overlap between immigrants and hosts is high. Second, immigrant leaders strike deals with local police to obtain protection in return for cooperation. Third, immigrant leaders punish immigrants who refuse to buy into these arrangements.

Immigrant community leaders know what type of ethnic and religious landscape their constituents fall into in their host societies, and are the first to point out how easy it might be for some to simply blend in, or "pass," as indigenous members of their host society. This is particularly prevalent for Hausa immigrants in Niamey, where Hausa is a shared ethnicity between citizens of Niger and immigrants from Nigeria; for Yoruba immigrants in Cotonou, where Yoruba is a shared ethnicity between citizens of Benin and immigrants from Nigeria; and for Christian Yoruba immigrants in Accra, where Christianity is a shared religion between Ghanaians in Accra and Yorubas.

In Niamey, the secretary general of the Association of Nigerian Citizens in Niger (ANCN), an Igbo, claims: "Sometimes, we cannot differentiate between a Nigerian Hausa and a Niger Hausa."[9] The public relations officer, himself a Hausa, explains that crossing the border into Niger is easy for Hausas "because of our common nature with the Hausas here in Niger ... if we don't speak, if they look at us in the face, they would not differentiate some Hausas from Niger as some Hausas from Nigeria."[10] When asked whether he speaks any local language in Niger, this interviewee affirms, "Yes, Hausa is a local language in Niger."[11] The Yoruba Chief in Niamey concurs with this position: "Nigeriens can't differentiate between Nigerian and Nigerien Hausas. But it's not the case for Yorubas."[12]

In Cotonou, the president of the Ede Youth Society, a Yoruba youth hometown association, asserts that "Anagos are the same as Yorubas, they are all from Nigeria. There is no difference between Anago and Yoruba."[13] One Yoruba foreign exchange trader in Cotonou's Jonquet neighborhood agrees that "Anagos are just like Yorubas but the language is a bit different."[14] The personal assistant to the president of the Nigerian Community Union (NCU) in Cotonou, an Igbo, explains that "if you are a Nigerian Yoruba, you can mingle with other Yorubas in Benin."[15] The general secretary of the NCU in Cotonou, a Yoruba, is also aware of the opportunities Nigerian Yorubas have to assimilate as Beninois Yorubas. His perception is that the

---

[9] Interview by the author with the secretary general of the Association of the Nigerian Citizens in Niamey, Niger: February 28, 2007.

[10] Interview by the author with the public relations officer of the Association of Nigerian Citizens in Niamey, Niger: March 2, 2007.

[11] Ibid.

[12] Interview by the author with the Yoruba chief in Niamey, Niger: September 27(B), 2007.

[13] Anago is a Yoruba subgroup, used primarily to denote Yorubas in Benin. Not all Beninois Yorubas, however, are Anagos; furthermore, not all Anagos are Beninois. In the interviews conducted with immigrant communities in Cotonou, however, respondents all assumed Anagos to be Beninois Yorubas, and employed the term Anago accordingly. Interview by the author in Cotonou, Benin: July 11(D), 2007.

[14] Interview by the author in Cotonou, Benin: July 12, 2007.

[15] Interview by the author with the personal assistant to the president of the Nigerian Community Union, Cotonou, Benin: August 22, 2007.

police "don't arrest Yorubas as much because there are Yorubas
here so they may think it's a Yoruba from Benin Republic."[16]

In Accra, where Christian Yorubas share a religion with Christian Accra, opportunities for immigrant defection also exist in
the eyes of Yoruba leaders. The pastor of the main Yoruba
Baptist Church in downtown Accra is indeed aware that his
Baptist Yoruba constituents are able to join indigenous Ghanaian churches: "Most Christian Yorubas in Ghana are Baptist. But
they are not all in this Church. There are other Yoruba Baptists
in indigenous churches: Calvary, Tesano Baptist Churches."[17]

Leaders of immigrant communities demonstrate a keen awareness of the opportunities immigrants face to tap into indigenous
networks for socioeconomic resources, and see them as a function
of the religions and ethnicities that immigrants and hosts share.
Even leaders of the Igbo community recognize that Yorubas and
Hausas encounter different ethno-religious landscapes in their
host societies, and that those landscapes shape the opportunities Yorubas and Hausas have to tap into a variety of different
cultural networks.[18]

A second fact we learn from conversations with immigrant
community leaders and with local police is that leaders strike
deals with local authorities: the police agree to let immigrant
leaders protect their loyal constituents from police harassment,
and immigrant leaders cooperate with local police by establishing
and maintaining order within their group. The Nigerian Embassy
Identity Card is one mechanism by which this deal is formalized

---

[16] Interview by the author with the secretary general of the Nigerian Community
Union in Cotonou, Benin: August 15, 2007.

[17] Interview with the pastor of Mark Hayford Memorial Baptist Church in Accra,
Ghana: February 2, 2007.

[18] We learn an additional fact from these interviews: it is probably and indeed
likely that some high-overlap immigrants are able to pass as indigenous and
fully incorporate into their host societies. The research method employed
here effectively misses out on that population of immigrants. This problem is
pervasive in any study of immigrant incorporation, which inevitably misses
those who successfully assimilate. The fact that successful assimilators exist
does not necessarily take away from the analysis here. It does, however, justify
the continued and persistent paranoia on the part of immigrant leaders, who
cannot be 100% successful in preventing immigrant assimilation and therefore
are rational in their continued fear of immigrant defection over time.

and enforced. The police recognize this card as a valid form of identity, and immigrant community leaders have the authority to facilitate access to this card.[19] The personal assistant to the president of the NCU in Cotonou explains that, "if you don't have the [embassy] ID card, the police can catch you anytime.... Before the card, the police arrested anybody. But now if you are arrested and you show them the card, they will leave you."[20] The president of the Association of Nigerian Citizens in Niamey, a Hausa, explains; "If somebody goes to jail or has a problem with the police, they show their embassy card. If it's not a criminal problem, the Nigerian community will come to his aid if he has the card."[21] One Yoruba foreign exchange trader born in Benin explains that the "police can stop you if they see you walking around at night – if you can't produce your card, they can take you to jail or to the border."[22] The Yoruba chief in Niamey also claims that the first thing authorities ask for is the identity card. He and members of his executive council always carry their embassy identity card with them.[23] An assistant to the pastor at the Yoruba Baptist Church in Accra explains that the church procured the card for all its members in 2002, after a peak in crime rates in Accra triggered mass police crackdowns on aliens.[24] A trader in Dantokpa market, the main market in Cotonou, asserts that he proudly has his Nigerian embassy identity card but no passport. He explains that "the police raids various places, and when you show the card you are left alone."[25]

The card is a necessary though insufficient method of protection for Nigerian immigrants. Indeed, the Nigerian embassy

---

[19] It is not impossible for individual immigrants to obtain the card on their own, but the process in this case is lengthier and more laborious (interview by the author, September 20(A), 2011).

[20] Interview by the author with the personal assistant to the president of the Nigerian Community Union, Cotonou, Benin: August 22, 2007.

[21] Interview by the author with the president of the Association of Nigerian Citizens in Niamey, Niger: September 27(A), 2007.

[22] Interview by the author in Cotonou, Benin: August 20, 2007.

[23] Interview by the author with the Yoruba chief and members of his executive council in Niamey, Niger: September 27(B), 2007.

[24] Interview by the author in Accra, Ghana: December 10, 2007.

[25] Interview by the author in Cotonou, Benin: July 11(C), 2007.

identity card did not always exist. Before membership was formalized through the purchase of the card, loyal members had to accrue social capital vis-à-vis their leaders in order to enjoy the club goods leaders had to offer. This informal mechanism remains salient today, because the police always retain a certain degree of discretion and may arrest even card-carrying members. The personal assistant to the president of the NCU in Cotonou confirms that the "[P]olice can still arrest you if you have the card if they want to intimidate you.... When an Igbo or a Nigerian is unjustly arrested (has not committed a crime), NCU leaders go to the police station and the police cooperates."[26] Individual immigrants who want to stay safe thus need not only acquire the card but also foster social capital with their leaders by signaling their commitment to their immigrant community organization beyond formal membership. This is true for two reasons. First, the identity card evidently does not protect immigrants entirely against police harassment; maintaining good relations with the immigrant community leader is an important complement to purchasing the identity card. Second, leaders can impose preconditions for purchasing the identity card. Because individual immigrants apply via their leader, leaders can choose to facilitate the process only for those who have built up enough social capital. In sum, immigrant community leaders foster key ties with the local police, and the police have the authority to intimidate even card-carrying members of an immigrant group: this induces immigrant commitment, both formal and informal, to their association.

Members of the local police confirm that they maintain important relations with leaders of immigrant communities, who help them identify "bad apples" if need be. The police enjoy collaborating with these leaders and know to trust them because "their credibility is at stake."[27] Indeed, according to the police chief of the 5th Arrondissement in Cotonou, the Nigerian embassy acts

---

[26] Interview by the author with the personal assistant to the president of the Nigerian Community Union, Cotonou, Benin: August 22, 2007.

[27] Interview with police chief, police station of the 5th Arrondissement in Cotonou, Benin: August 24, 2007.

as guarantor of relations between local police and immigrant leaders: it ensures that community leaders remain credible and cooperate with the police. In Cotonou's 5th Arrondissement, the chief of police cannot recall a single instant when immigrant community leaders refused to cooperate.

Finally, interviews with immigrant community leaders indicate that leaders shun immigrants who have no embassy identity card. The secretary general of the Nigerian Community Union in Cotonou explains that "if you are arrested without your ID card, I may not even intervene."[28] The president of the Nigerian Community Union in Niamey further explicates that "you can't get anything from the Nigerian Embassy without that card. If you want a business, an account, have children in school, anything that has to do with authority, you have to have the card."[29] The PRO of the Association of Nigerian Citizens in Niamey laments that many Nigerians do not pay their annual membership fee, and that they come only when they are in need of their identity card. He explains that the association counters this by restricting access to the identity card to members who already have their union association card. This is, according to him, a good strategy for inducing immigrant commitment to their community associations, because "if the police stop you, you need the ID card on you."[30]

Immigrant Attachment to Immigrant Communities

This chapter claims that immigrant leaders have an incentive to enforce individual immigrant commitment to the organizations they lead when they fear immigrant defection stemming from cultural overlap. Leaders do so through stricter enforcement of formal and informal member attachment to their immigrant association. Furthermore, immigrants abide by these conditions in

---

[28] Interview by the author with the secretary general of the Nigerian Community Union, Cotonou, Benin: August 15, 2007.

[29] Interview by the author with the president of the Nigerian Community Union, Niamey, Niger: September 27(A), 2007.

[30] Interview by the author with the public relations office of the Association of the Nigerian Citizens in Niamey, Niger: March 2, 2007.

order to access critical group benefits that keep them financially and socially secure. The preceding section surveyed immigrant community leaders in their own words and found evidence of their incentives and strategies for inducing immigrant community attachment, particularly for high-overlap immigrants. In evaluating the strategies leaders use to protect their benefits, and the incentives immigrants have to abide, we also expect to observe greater formal and informal attachment to immigrant associations on the part of high-overlap immigrants relative to low-overlap immigrants.

Such a test can be carried out using results from the immigrant community survey administered to an availability sample of Nigerian Hausas and Yorubas in Accra, Cotonou, and Niamey in 2007. Specifically, comparing levels on the immigrant attachment index for each group in each city is illustrative. This index is constructed as an average of nine indicators of attachment to the immigrant community, each expressed as a value between 0 and 1 that increases with immigrant attachment: (1) percent who traveled back to Nigeria over the previous month; (2) percent who voted in the last Nigerian presidential elections; (3) percent who currently send remittances back to Nigeria; (4) percent who have tribal marks; (5) percent who acquired their current job through the help of a coethnic; (6) percent whose children are schooled only in Nigeria; (7) percent who hold a Nigerian passport; (8) percent who follow the Nigerian news daily; and (9) percent who self-identify as Nigerian over host country national.[31]

Figure 2.1 provides a sense of the average trends in immigrant in-group attachment by host city. For each host city, immigrant groups are ordered from left to right by increasing level of cultural overlap.[32] Each bar illustrates the average score on

[31] See Appendix B for the construction of this index.
[32] Cultural overlap is operationalized as a dichotomous variable: in each host city, one group is relatively low-overlap and the other is relatively high-overlap. The analysis can also be done using a continuous measure of cultural overlap, as the product of the share of each population that shares a cultural trait (ethnicity or religion – see Appendix C). This does not change which group is relatively low-overlap and which is relatively high-overlap. The dichotomous measure used here better illustrates the patterns.

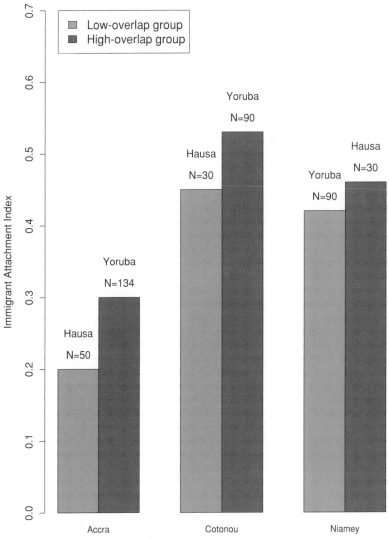

FIGURE 2.1. Average immigrant group attachment by ethnicity and host city

immigrant-group attachment for each immigrant group. Hence, higher levels on the index indicate greater levels of immigrant attachment to the immigrant community.

Figure 2.1 indicates that groups with higher cultural overlap, on average, score higher on immigrant attachment than do groups with lower cultural overlap. In Accra and Cotonou, where Yorubas share greater overlap than Hausas, Yorubas display greater attachment to their community than do Hausas. In Niamey, however, where Hausas share greater overlap than Yorubas, Hausas display greater attachment to their community than do Yorubas. Furthermore, groups that share both an ethnicity and a religion with their host communities consistently display the highest levels of attachment. Hausa immigrants in Niamey share not only an ethnicity with their host society but also a religion. This means they have countless opportunities to blend in with Niger's indigenous population, through a shared language, a shared ethnic identity, a shared religious identity, or shared religious institutions. Yet their level of attachment to their immigrant community is higher than that of the Yorubas in Niamey and as high as, or higher than, that of Hausas elsewhere. The same pattern holds for Yorubas in Cotonou, who share both an ethnicity and a religion with their host population. They exhibit the highest level of community attachment for all immigrant groups. This counterintuitive result supports the implications of the argument: immigrants who face the most opportunities to cross the alien-indigenous boundary and tap into indigenous networks demonstrate the strongest attachment to their immigrant group. Conversely, immigrants facing the fewest opportunities to tap into indigenous networks – that is, the Hausas in Accra – demonstrate the weakest attachment to their group.

Figure 2.1 is remarkable not only because it confirms the patterns predicted by the argument within each host locality but also because it illustrates patterns that are consistent with the argument's prediction for the same ethnic group, across each host locality. For example, the immigrant attachment index for Hausas increases with the Hausa level of cultural overlap across Accra, Cotonou, and Niamey. In Accra, where Hausas share close to no cultural traits with Ghanaians, the index is lowest. In Cotonou, where Hausas share a religion with Beninois society, the index is higher. Finally, in Niamey, where Hausas share both a religion and an ethnicity, the index is highest. The same is true for Yorubas across Accra, Cotonou, and Niamey. In Accra, where half of the Yoruba community shares a religion with Ghanaians, the index is lowest. In Niamey, where the largely Muslim Yoruba community shares a religion with Nigeriens, the index is higher. Finally, in Cotonou, where Yorubas share a religion and an ethnicity with Beninois society, the index is highest. Therefore, even after controlling for the ethnic identity of the immigrant group, immigrant attachment correlates positively with cultural overlap.[33]

Beyond these general patterns, this analysis looks at disaggregated patterns of formal and informal attachment as well. Indicators of informal attachment to the immigrant community include (1) where immigrants choose to send their children to school, (2) the extent to which they self-identify as Nigerian (versus Ghanaian, Beninois, or Nigerien), and (3) the frequency of travel back to Nigeria. Indicators of formal attachment to the immigrant community include (1) the extent to which immigrants know the name of their community leader, (2) the extent to which they continue to vote in Nigerian presidential elections, and (3) the proportion of immigrants with a Nigerian passport.

Informal indicators suggest that immigrants who share cultural traits with their host society tend to exhibit greater commitment to their own community in their everyday individual decisions. Table 2.1 summarizes how Yorubas and Hausas in each host city score on a sample of informal indicators. To facilitate interpretation, immigrant groups in each host city are ordered from left to right by increasing degree of cultural overlap, with

---

[33] Although beyond the scope of this study, it is interesting to note the differences in immigrant attachment across cities more generally. In Accra, both Yoruba and Hausa immigrants show less attachment than in Cotonou and Niamey. This may be a sign that immigrants are, in general, better integrated in cities that are more economically dynamic.

TABLE 2.1. *Informal Indicators of Attachment by Ethnicity and Host City*

	Accra		Cotonou		Niamey	
	Hausa	Yoruba	Hausa	Yoruba	Yoruba	Hausa
Percentage who sent their children to school only in Nigeria	4%	10%	33%	31%	20%	27%
Percentage who identify as Nigerian (over Ghanaian, Beninois, or Nigerien, respectively)	6%	53%	73%	96%	91%	90%
Percentage who traveled back to Nigeria in the previous month	4%	11%	27%	32%	4%	23%

the low-overlap group in the left-hand column and the high-overlap group in the right-hand column. The figures in bold are consistent with the implications of the argument.

Table 2.1 indicates that high-overlap groups are more likely to school their children in Nigeria, identify as Nigerian, and travel back to their homeland. Two exceptions lie with the extent to which Hausas and Yorubas in Niamey identify as "Nigerian" and with the extent to which Hausas and Yorubas in Cotonou school their children in Nigeria. The groups hold similar scores for these two indicators. Overall, however, high-overlap groups tend to display greater attachment than do low-overlap groups.

Formal indicators further suggest that immigrants who share cultural traits with their host society also tend to exhibit greater attachment to their group organizations. Table 2.2 summarizes how Yorubas and Hausas in each host city score on a sample of formal indicators. To facilitate interpretation, immigrant groups in each host city are ordered from left to right by increasing degree of cultural overlap, and figures in bold are consistent with the theory's predictions.

Table 2.2 indicates that high-overlap groups tend to exhibit greater formal attachment to their organization than do low-overlap groups. Indeed, high-overlap groups consistently vote in Nigerian elections with greater frequency than do low-overlap

TABLE 2.2. *Formal Indicators of Attachment by Ethnicity and Host City*

	Accra		Cotonou		Niamey	
	Hausa	Yoruba	Hausa	Yoruba	Yoruba	Hausa
Percentage who know the name of the president of the Nigerian community organization in their host city	N/A	N/A	3%	10%	13%	53%
Percentage who voted in the last Nigerian presidential elections	6%	16%	33%	57%	11%	30%
Percentage who hold a Nigerian passport	6%	37%	7%	31%	39%	30%

groups. They also are more likely to know the name of the Nigerian community president in their host city.[34] Finally, although data on Nigerian passports are less conclusive, they are informative nonetheless. Indeed, given how rarely Hausas tend to hold a Nigerian passport elsewhere, it is remarkable that a third of them do in Niamey.[35]

The Christian and Muslim Yorubas in Accra and Niamey

The Yoruba community in Accra provides a further opportunity to test the book's central argument. Approximately 40 percent

---

[34] It is important to recognize that the fact that the president of the Nigerian community organization in Niamey is a Hausa may explain why Hausas in Niamey are more likely to know who he is. Two additional pieces of information, however, suggest that the result in Table 2.2 is more than just an artifact of Hausas knowing their own. First, only 30% of Yorubas knew that he was a Hausa, meaning that 43% of Yorubas in Niamey either knew who the president was or that he was Hausa – this number is still ten percentage points less than the 53% of Hausas who knew who he was. Second, only 26% of Yorubas in Niamey knew the name of their Yoruba chief. Overall, these figures indicate that, in Niamey, Hausas are more aware of their formal leadership than are Yorubas. This issue is not relevant in Cotonou, where the president of the Nigerian Community Organization is an Igbo.

[35] Data on knowing the name of the president of the Nigerian Community Organization were not collected in Accra, Ghana.

of Yorubas in Nigeria are Muslim and 60 percent are Christian.[36] Furthermore, the immigrant Yoruba community in Accra appears to have reproduced this cleavage, since both Christian and Muslim Yorubas have settled in Ghana's capital in significant numbers. In fact, of the 134 Yorubas surveyed in Accra, approximately 56 percent are Christian and 44 percent are Muslim.[37] It is therefore possible to apply the argument in this chapter to the Christian and Muslim Yoruba immigrants in Christian Accra. If leaders of high-overlap immigrant groups are more likely to highlight group boundaries, we expect to find greater attachment to immigrant communities among the Christian Yorubas than among the Muslim Yorubas.

A variety of sources confirm that while Christian Yorubas organized around formal institutions, Muslim Yorubas did not. Sudarkasa (1979) explains that the Parapo did not take hold until the 1920s, when large waves of Christian Yoruba immigrants arrived in Ghana. The Parapo became the Yoruba's main institutional mechanism for maintaining in-group cohesion once these Christian Yorubas arrived in Kumasi.[38] Furthermore, the Yoruba Baptist Church has played a critical role for the organization of Christian Yorubas in Ghana. Its members express a strong preference for being among Yorubas during their worship service: "Since I am a Yoruba and we Yorubas have our own Church.... I like interacting with my Yoruba people."[39] The Yoruba Baptist Church in Accra has always been known as the Nigerian Church. By contrast, Muslim Yorubas do not organize as a distinct ethnic entity through their religious institutions. A leading scholar on immigration into Ghana confirms this distinction between Muslim and Christian institutions in Ghana:

---

[36] See Laitin (1986).

[37] This is not the case for the Yorubas sampled in Cotonou and Niamey: many more Muslim Yorubas were sampled relative to Christian Yorubas.

[38] Interviews with Christian Yorubas in Accra confirm that the most active town union is the Ogbomosho Parapo, a predominantly Christian Nigerian town (interviews, Accra: January 29(A), 2007 and February 5(A), 2007).

[39] Interview, Accra: February 5(A), 2007.

Muslims go to any mosque. Every community has its own mosque, but there are also bigger mosques where everybody congregates during Friday prayers. Every day there are small prayer places in every small community; an enclave of Hausas in a neighborhood can have their own small places, where they pray daily. But on Friday they want to go to a big mosque. In Christianity, there are several denominations and Christians organize themselves along such denominations. Sects in Islam have not come out as denominations; it looks like there is a deliberate attempt to keep these divisions minimal. These sects do not operate as autonomous bodies. They all go to the same mosque.[40]

One leader of the Yoruba Muslim community in Accra echoes that "when it comes to Mosque, you don't [specify] Nigerian, Ghanaian – we are Muslim, we are Muslim."[41] Another member of the Yoruba youth, when asked which mosque he belongs to, retorts: "Any mosque belongs to Muslims... any mosque, you can pray. It's not like the Christians, when you are at this church you're supposed to be at that church, no. The Muslims, when they call the prayers, you hear, you can join them anywhere... The Yorubas have their own church."[42] Consequently, as one interviewee claims, "Muslim Yorubas mixed with Hausas, closer with Hausas than with Christian Yorubas."[43] A prominent Muslim Yoruba living in Accra claims that Muslims "believe that if you are a Muslim, whether you are a Ga, an Ashanti, you are white, you are black: we are one!"[44]

My own surveys with Christian and Muslim Yorubas in Accra corroborate these patterns. Figure 2.2 illustrates the average level of immigrant community attachment for low-overlap Muslim Yorubas (left) and high-overlap Christian Yorubas (right). It

---

[40] Interview, Accra: January 18(A), 2007.
[41] Interview, Accra: January 24(B), 2007.
[42] Interview, Accra: February 7(A), 2007.
[43] Interview, Accra: April 29, 2007.
[44] Interview, Accra: January 24(B), 2007. This section is not meant to portray the Muslim community in Accra as unified. Pellow (1985) documents and demonstrates that the Muslim community in Accra was and is neither homogenous nor unified. The argument in this chapter is a relative one: the Christian Yorubas organize as a separate ethnic Christian community while Muslim Yorubas mix with the Muslim community of Accra.

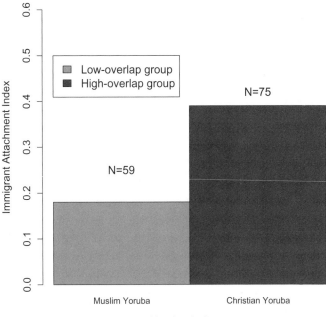

FIGURE 2.2. Average Yoruba attachment in Accra

indicates a substantial difference (approximately twenty-one percentage points) in attachment between the two groups, with the
high-overlap Christian Yorubas largely overwhelming the low-
overlap Muslim Yorubas in immigrant group attachment.

Table 2.3 summarizes the values on each sample of informal and formal indicators for Muslim and Christian Yorubas
in Accra. Note, however, that data on the name of the Nigerian Association president were not collected among immigrant
communities in Accra. Two indicators that shed light on differ-
ing attachment levels between Christian and Muslim Yorubas in
Accra are thus added. The first is the extent to which a Yoruba
identifies with his ethnicity (Yoruba) rather than his religion
(Christian/Muslim). If leaders highlight group boundaries successfully, then we expect high-overlap Christian Yorubas to identify as Yoruba (ethnicity, the nonoverlapping trait) over Christian

TABLE 2.3. *Disaggregated Indicators of Yoruba Attachment in Accra*

	Accra	
	Muslim Yoruba	Christian Yoruba
Percentage who sent or send their children to school only in Nigeria	7%	13%
Percentage who identify as Nigerian (over Ghanaian)	24%	76%
Percentage who traveled back to Nigeria in the previous month	8%	13%
Percentage who voted in the last Nigerian presidential elections	5%	24%
Percentage who hold a Nigerian passport	14%	56%
Percentage who identify with their ethnicity (Yoruba) rather than their religion	10%	20%
Percentage who support Nigeria in a soccer match against Ghana	35%	90%

(religion, the overlapping trait) with more frequency than Muslim Yorubas, who may not face the same incentives to signal their attachment to one or the other identity dimension. Given that Muslim and Christian Yorubas are both Yoruba, this indicator is useful in conveying the strength of one identity category over another. The second variable indicates which soccer team an immigrant will support in a game between the Ghanaian and Nigerian national teams. This question is more significant than we might otherwise imagine. Soccer is the most popular sport in Ghana, especially given the success of Ghanaian players in international soccer leagues. Nigeria has historically enjoyed a strong national record in the sport as well. A face-off between the two represents a face-off between two equally strong teams, and involves questions of national pride.[45]

The data in Table 2.4 indicate that Christian Yorubas tend to maintain greater informal and formal attachment to their

[45] This question is less relevant in Benin or Niger, where national teams have performed relatively poorly.

TABLE 2.4. *Associational Trends of Yorubas and Hausas in Accra in 2007*

Type of Organization	Hausas	Muslim Yorubas	Christian Yorubas
Religion only	18%	11.86%	4%
Ethnicity only	2%	8.47%	21.33%
Religion and Ethnicity	14%	13.56%	2.67%

community than do Muslim Yorubas. Christian Yorubas exhibit greater in-group attachment for every indicator listed. The differences in self-identification are especially striking: 76 percent of Christian Yorubas, compared to only 24 percent of Muslim Yorubas, identify as Nigerian rather than Ghanaian.[46] Furthermore, 20 percent of Christian Yorubas, compared to 10 percent of Muslim Yorubas, identify with their ethnicity – the cultural trait that does not overlap with Accra society – rather than their religion. Finally, the divergent loyalties in soccer are striking. While 90 percent of Christian Yorubas support their Nigerian team, only 35 percent of Muslim Yorubas do.

Christian Yorubas therefore seem to prioritize their ethnic identity when it comes to organizing: they come together as Christians only insofar as they are with other Yorubas. Muslim Yorubas and Hausas, on the other hand, prioritize their religion over their ethnic affiliation, and come together by ethnicity only insofar as they are with other Muslims. The survey data summarized above indicate that these patterns persist to this day. Furthermore, an overview of the primary community organizations of which Hausa and Yoruba survey respondents are members reveals that Hausas and Muslim Yorubas are unlikely to belong to solely ethnic organizations and much more likely to organize around religion; Christian Yorubas, on the other hand, are more likely to organize around only their ethnic community.[47] Indeed,

[46] This result holds even when we control for place of birth. Among those born in Ghana, just under 14% of Muslim Yorubas (N = 51) identify as Nigerian over Ghanaian, compared with close to 60% of Christian Yorubas (N = 32).

[47] Community organizations are coded by type as follows: "religion only" types are organizations whose membership is multiethnic but monoreligious; "ethnicity only" types are organizations whose membership is monoethnic but

whereas 18 percent of Hausas and close to 12 percent of Muslim Yorubas belong to religious associations, only 4 percent of Christian Yorubas do. By contrast, whereas more than 21 percent of Christian Yorubas belong to ethnic associations, slightly more than 8 percent of Muslim Yorubas and only 2 percent of Hausas do.

The Yoruba community in Accra is far from monolithic. It exhibits important differences in both formal and informal signs of immigrant community attachment, based on religion. These results are consistent with this chapter's main argument, that high-overlap immigrant groups (Christian Yorubas) display greater attachment to their immigrant community than do low-overlap immigrant groups (Muslim Yorubas).

The Incentive to Resist Assimilation

So far, this chapter has argued and provided evidence showing that Yorubas display greater attachment to their immigrant community than do Hausas, and that Christian Yorubas display greater attachment than do Muslim Yorubas. But what of the incentives underlying such behavior? How can we be sure that immigrant groups behave this way because of the incentive to resist assimilation? The argument in this book presupposes that it is this desire to resist assimilation, rather than pull factors back home, that drives differential patterns of immigrant group attachment between Yorubas and Hausas. This section relies on interview data with Yoruba migrants in Ghana to reveal the incentives behind the adoption of such potentially costly behavior.

In their interviews, Christian Yorubas express an acute awareness of a need to preserve their distinct identity through language and culture. One Christian Yoruba interviewee, who resides in Ghana, has sent all his children back to Nigeria: "I want them to understand the Yoruba culture, speak the language more."[48] Another, who lives in Kumasi, explains that her parents sent her

---

multireligious; "religion and ethnicity" types are organizations whose membership is both monoethnic and monoreligious. The organization's ethnic and religious composition is based on the respondent's own assessment.

[48] Interview, Accra: February 5(A), 2007.

back to Ogbomosho, Nigeria (her hometown, although she was born in Tamale, Ghana), to complete her primary school because "[t]hey want me to know our tradition...they want me to hear Yoruba."[49] Other Christian Yorubas were sent back to Nigeria by their parents to learn Yoruba or attend school in Yorubaland.[50]

Muslim Yorubas and Hausas, by contrast, do not express the same desire or need to preserve their distinct identity. Hausas and Muslim Yorubas in Ghana express instead a certain pride in assimilating into Ghanaian society. Hausas, for instance, recognize that the Hausa community is "not as tight-knit as the Yoruba community"[51] and that the Hausa "easily gets lost."[52] They also assert that Ghana has its own Hausa ethnic group, a claim that reveals a loose conception of the Hausa ethnicity based mainly on a shared religion or language between northern Nigerians and northern Ghanaians. Similarly, Muslim Yorubas proudly refer to the well-known intermarriage of the prominent Brimah (Muslim Yoruba) and Peregrino (Ga – the indigenous ethnicity of Accra) families in Accra as evidence that Muslim Yorubas are well established in Accra. They often claim that the Ga, the founding ethnic group of Accra, originally migrated from Ile-Ife in Nigeria.[53] In fact, a common expression that Muslim Yorubas have used in their interviews is that "We came here in the morning, these people [the Ga] came here in the afternoon."[54] In contrast to Christian Yorubas, who are proud of their efforts to preserve their distinct culture, Muslim Yorubas and Hausas tend to flaunt their ability to assimilate. One young Muslim Yoruba leader in Accra proudly exclaims: "I was born here, I educate here, I do my everything here."[55] Another Christian Yoruba explains that Hausas settle in the Zongo quarters and forget where they come

[49] Interview, Accra: February 6(A), 2007.
[50] Interviews, Accra: February 6(B), 2007; February 13(A), 2007.
[51] Interview, Accra: January 29(B), 2007.
[52] Interview, Accra: April 28, 2007.
[53] Interviews, Accra: January 24(B), 2007; February 7(A), 2007.
[54] Interview, Accra: February 7(A), 2007.
[55] Interview, Accra: February 7(A), 2007.

from in Nigeria, which is why they have come to integrate with Ghanaians.[56] Yet another explains: "As for Hausas, when they come to a country and they are well established, they don't go back... they don't normally go to where they come from."[57]

Not a single interviewee expressed a desire to return to Nigeria because of the pull of socioeconomic opportunities back home. Those who offered a reason for resisting assimilation always did so using a cultural explanation, emphasizing the need to preserve one's identity. In sum, interviews with members of the Hausa and Yoruba communities display contrasting incentives between a Christian Yoruba community investing in the maintenance of a distinct identity and a Muslim Yoruba and Hausa community proud of its ability to lose itself in the society in which it has settled.

2.4 Conclusion

In this chapter I have shown that cultural overlap between immigrants and their hosts results in slower absorption of immigrant communities, not more rapid assimilation. This is so because of the strategies immigrant leaders employ to preserve their positions, and the incentives individual immigrants have to comply. Using interview data, this chapter has shown that immigrant community leaders are aware of, and threatened by, the shared cultural traits that provide individual immigrants with opportunities to tap into indigenous cultural networks and thus decrease their dependence on their leaders as monopoly providers of socioeconomic security. Using survey data, this chapter has further shown that high-overlap immigrants signal greater formal and informal attachment to their immigrant communities than do low-overlap immigrants. These findings hold even when controlling for an immigrant's ethnicity. Finally, using interview data, this chapter has explored the incentives behind differential patterns of attachment and demonstrated that the desire to maintain a distinct identity versus the desire to assimilate, not pull

---

[56] Interview, Accra: February 5(B), 2007.
[57] Interview, Accra: February 6(B), 2007.

factors back home, drives the outcomes observed. The findings in this chapter suggest that the ethno-religious landscapes immigrant communities settle into carry significant consequences for the degree of attachment immigrants retain with their communities. Yet they also raise a new issue: How do host societies react to immigrants with whom they share cultural traits? The next chapter addresses this question.

.

3

Immigrant Exclusion from Host Societies

"Yorubas eat people." My Accra taxi driver had inquired about my research on my commute home from work, and interrupted my account when I told him I was working with Yoruba and Hausa communities. He further explained that Yorubas are Nigerians, that they are fraudsters, perform black magic, and cannot be trusted. Hausas, on the other hand, did not evoke the same agitation: "Hausas are Ghanaians," he shrugged.[1] Although blunt, my taxi driver expressed sentiments I had already heard in one form or another among Ghanaians in Accra.

This chapter asks whether and why urban African immigrants who share cultural similarities with their host societies face greater exclusion than those who share no such cultural similarities. The previous chapter showed that immigrants who share cultural traits with their host societies display greater attachment to their immigrant communities; in this chapter, I demonstrate that those immigrant groups also experience greater exclusion from their hosts. This is so because indigenous merchants are directly threatened by the implications of cultural overlap and increase their hostility toward groups who they perceive can more easily assimilate through the cultural networks they share with their host societies.

---

[1] Conversation in Accra, Ghana: April 2007.

In this chapter I first elaborate the argument that cultural overlap increases economic competition between immigrants and hosts, and thus elicits greater exclusionary attitudes among hosts. I then test the argument using survey data on a random sample of Ghanaians in Accra and Nigeriens in Niamey. I further test the argument with a comparative analysis of immigrant insecurity among Christian and Muslim Yorubas in Ghana at the time of Ghana's Alien Compliance Order of 1969. Finally, I survey prominent alternative explanations for why Yorubas are more excluded in Accra while Hausas are more excluded in Niamey, and show that these do not pan out.

3.1 Immigrant Exclusion in Urban West Africa

Immigrant traders compete for resources – like customers and supplies – with indigenous merchants in the urban centers in which they settle. Indigenous merchants have an advantage over their immigrant counterparts: they are indigenous, and this yields important benefits in urban African settings. First, it offers security in a context lacking formal-legal institutions that can define a clear path to citizenship and protect immigrants from the whims of local politicians and enforcement agents. Second, it offers access to indigenous networks of customers, loan associations, and supplies. Urban immigrant merchants, too, benefit from their immigrant networks of customers, loan associations, and supplies. But their nonindigenous status means that they operate in fear of police and social harassment. No matter how legal the immigrant's status, the weakness of formal-legal channels of immigrant incorporation implies that enforcement agents retain just enough discretion to render an immigrant's nonindigenous origins a real liability.

Yet the flip side of this informal process is the relative ease with which an immigrant might cross the informal indigenous-alien boundary: indeed, legal and administrative obstacles to passing as a member of the indigenous population are largely absent in these contexts. Immigrants can use, and indeed have used strategies ranging from speaking the local language to changing their manner of dress in order to pass as indigenous in the eyes of the police. In Ghana in November 1969, for example, when Prime Minister Busia decreed an Alien Compliance Order giving all undocumented aliens two weeks to regularize their status or leave the country, a number of Nigerian immigrants switched their type of dress and spoke only the local Twi or Ga languages in order to protect themselves.[2]

But an immigrant who can access indigenous economic resources via her cultural repertoire is an immigrant who can compete more effectively with her hosts. Competition over scarce resources involves exclusion. For example, Fearon (1999) explains that the distribution of political pork tends to create "a strong incentive to limit the size of the winning coalition in order not to dilute each winner's share of the spoils."[3] The sociology literature on intergroup conflict makes a similar claim that fundamental competition over real economic resources determines negative attitudes toward immigrants: attitudes toward immigrants are consequences of a perceived zero-sum game where greater access to resources by one group means less for the individual and his group.[4] In West Africa, access to scarce resources means access to civil security and informal economic networks; immigrant groups who can obtain access to such resources through shared cultural networks thus pose an acute competitive threat to their hosts.

This argument finds a parallel in the most recent literature on interethnic cooperation and conflict, where economic

---

[2] Interviews in Accra, Ghana: January 28(B), 2007; February 7(B), 2007; February 12(A), 2007. As noted in Chapter 2, passing as indigenous is not a rational individual immigrant strategy. It may happen at the margins, or in a time of crisis – as in Ghana's 1969 mass immigrant expulsion – but it is not the dominant strategy for individual immigrants otherwise. What matters here, however, is not whether or not immigrants actually try to pass, but rather the perception indigenous merchants have about immigrants' ability to pass.

[3] Fearon (1999): 5. See also Gradstein and Schiff (2006).

[4] See, for example, Esses et al. (1998); Levine and Campbell (1972); Olzak (1992); Sears and McConahy (1973).

complementarity breeds ethnic cooperation while economic competition aggravates interethnic conflict. In an analysis of Hindu-Muslim relations in India, Jha (2007) finds that localities where Hindu and Muslim economic activities are substitutes for one another are the ones that have experienced interethnic conflict; by contrast, where Hindu and Muslim economic activities complement one another – namely in medieval port cities – Hindus and Muslims have coexisted relatively peaceably. In a large-N quantitative study of middleman minorities, Jeon (2011) demonstrates that middleman minorities, who tend to offer complementary economic activities in their host societies, are associated with less conflict compared to other minority groups in the same country. Jeon argues that this is indeed attributable to the complementarities such middleman minorities bring to the table. The argument in this chapter is not unlike these lines of thinking: urban immigrant traders who can use their cultural repertoires to access supplies, loans, or customers in their host societies pose a direct competitive threat to urban indigenous traders. This economic threat provokes hostility and exclusion.

Conversely, immigrant communities that are easily marked as foreigners because they share little to no cultural overlap with their hosts already face natural barriers to assimilation. With high natural barriers to entry, hosts do not perceive such communities as posing a viable challenge to the current distribution of resources.[5] Hence, immigrants with low cultural overlap with their hosts cannot use their cultural repertoires to access indigenous resources like security, customer networks, or loans. They pose less of a direct threat to urban indigenous hosts. Consequently, and rather counterintuitively, they experience less exclusion.

---

[5] In fact, Gradstein and Schiff (2006) suggest that such communities, in some circumstances, may actually be appealing to the host majority if they align themselves with an indigenous minority, because they shift the relative distribution of benefits in favor of a now relatively smaller majority: "Suppose that the immigrants belong to the minority ethnic group. Immigration, by increasing the size of the excluded minority, makes the majority better off" (Gradstein and Schiff 2006: 341).

3.2 The Face of Exclusion

This chapter tests the argument that hosts in urban West Africa exclude high-overlap immigrants more than they exclude low-overlap immigrants, using random sample surveys of Ghanaians in Accra and of Nigeriens in Niamey. In Accra, Yorubas are high-overlap while Hausas are low-overlap; Niamey presents the opposite scenario, with Yorubas as low-overlap immigrants and Hausas as high-overlap immigrants. How do Ghanaians in Accra and Nigeriens in Niamey react to the possible incorporation of these two non-indigenous ethnic groups?

Ghanaian Exclusion of Yorubas and Hausas in Accra

Which immigrant group do Ghanaians in Accra exclude? In Accra, Ghanaians were asked about their attitudes of exclusion and inclusion toward Yorubas and Hausas. Half of the Yoruba population of Accra is Christian while the other half is Muslim. The Hausa community in Accra, by contrast, is entirely Muslim. Given that Accra is an overwhelmingly Christian city, Yorubas share a religious overlap with their hosts that Hausas lack.

Figure 3.1 illustrates the average patterns of exclusionary attitudes of Ghanaians toward Yorubas and Hausas. It indicates a difference of twenty-four percentage points between Ghanaians' willingness to vote for a Hausa (31.58%) and their willingness to vote for a Yoruba (7.29%). It further indicates a twenty-three percentage-point difference between Ghanaians' beliefs that other Ghanaians would vote for a Hausa (32.63%) and their beliefs that other Ghanaians would vote for a Yoruba (9.38%). These differences-of-means are significant at the 99.9 percent confidence level in both one-tailed and two-tailed tests.

Do differences in exclusionary attitudes toward Yorubas and Hausas result from the fact that the sample of Ghanaians who answered the Yoruba questionnaire is different from the sample of Ghanaians who answered the Hausa questionnaire? Table 3.1 provides summary statistics for each sample population. It indicates that the average differences between the two samples are trivial, and balance tests confirm that none of these averages are

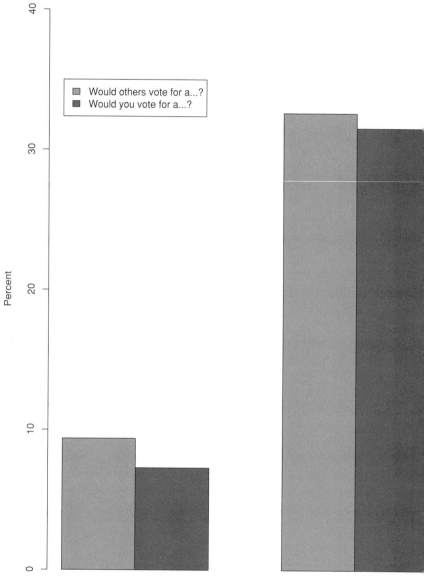

FIGURE 3.1. Exclusionary attitudes toward Yorubas and Hausas among Ghanaians in Accra

TABLE 3.1. *Summary Statistics for Ghanaian Respondents in Accra*

	Hausa Questionnaire		Yoruba Questionnaire	
	Mean	St. Deviation	Mean	St. Deviation
Sex (male = 1)	0.45	0.50	0.43	0.50
Age	38.01	12.55	37.81	12.7
Ga ethnicity	0.22	0.42	0.23	0.42
Ewe ethnicity	0.24	0.43	0.25	0.44
Akan ethnicity	0.54	0.50	0.52	0.50
Enumerator	0.50	0.50	0.51	0.50
Years lived in Accra	25.39	17.37	26.57	16.82
Nigerian area	0.58	0.50	0.58	0.50
Unemployed	0.04	0.20	0.06	0.24
Trader	0.50	0.50	0.56	0.50
Student	0	0	0.02	0.14
Observations	96		96	

statistically significantly different from each other. This reflects the fact that Hausa and Yoruba questionnaires were randomly distributed among participants.[6]

Nevertheless, in order to more precisely estimate the effect of receiving the Yoruba versus the Hausa questionnaire on Ghanaians' exclusionary attitudes, the following model is estimated:

$$ProbAffirmative_i = a + b_Y(Yoruba_i) + \mathbf{b_X X_i} + e_i \qquad (3.1)$$

where i is the Ghanaian respondent, *ProbAffirmative* is the probability that a respondent answers "yes" to the question "Do you

---

[6] Note, however, that the sample of indigenous merchants in Accra is heavily Christian: 188 respondents identified their religion as Christian, 2 as Animist and 2 as Muslim. This is because survey enumerators were instructed to focus on recruiting Akan, Ga, and Ewe respondents. These instructions were meant to ensure that only indigenous Ghanaian ethnic groups would be surveyed; but as a consequence, Christians are over represented, since most Akan, Ga, and Ewe are Christian. Indeed, Afrobarometer data for Ghana in 2005 indicate that the Muslim population of Accra is 9.78% (Afrobarometer 2005), as opposed to the 1% sampled here. This bias forbids an analysis of exclusionary attitudes among Muslim Ghanaians in Accra and limits the generalizability of the results to some extent, but it does not affect their internal validity.

believe Ghanaians would vote for a Yoruba (Hausa)?", *Yoruba* is a dummy variable for whether the respondent received the Yoruba or the Hausa questionnaire, and X is a vector of control variables from Table 3.1.

In Table 3.2, Models (1) through (5) estimate Equation 3.1. The independent variable of interest is Yoruba, a dummy variable that takes the value "1" if the respondent received the Yoruba questionnaire, and "0" if the respondent received the Hausa questionnaire. The basic model (1) confirms the difference-of-means results analyzed above: respondents are less likely to believe that Ghanaians would vote for a Yoruba than for a Hausa. In models (2) through (5), a number of key control variables are added.

Model (2) considers the effect of demographic factors, such as a respondent's sex, age, or ethnic identity (the baseline ethnic group is *Akan*), on the likelihood of excluding a Yoruba or a Hausa. Model (3) accounts for the enumerator bias that stems from the fact that two enumerators executed the survey and may have elicited different responses based on factors that cannot be observed.[7] Model (4) includes measures of a respondent's "cosmopolitanism," or the respondent's exposure to people of different ethnicities or nationalities. Modernization theory might predict that higher education, for example, decreases exclusionary attitudes (Lipset 1959; Hainmueller and Hiscox 2007). Furthermore, the model accounts for the number of years a respondent has lived in the capital city. If living in Accra exposes an individual to a greater diversity of people, or if more tolerant individuals are more likely to move to the capital at an early age, we might find less exclusionary attitudes in individuals who have been residents of Accra for longer periods of time. Finally, the model

---

[7] Alternatively, enumerators may have elicited different responses based on factors that are observable, such as their sex. Here, since one enumerator was male (coded as "0") and the other female (coded as "1"), results suggest that the female enumerator consistently elicited more exclusionary attitudes on the part of Ghanaians than did the male enumerator. However, since a number of unobservable factors may come into play, this statement is merely speculative.

TABLE 3.2. *Probability of an Affirmative Answer to: "Do You Think Ghanaians Would Vote for a Yoruba/Hausa?"*

	Model (1)	Model (2)	Model (3)	Model (4)	Model (5)
Yoruba	−1.544***	−1.552***	−1.591***	−1.549***	−1.582***
	(0.414)	(0.413)	(0.440)	(0.453)	(0.468)
Demographic					
Sex		0.179	0.218	0.283	0.437
		(0.374)	(0.373)	(0.384)	(0.461)
Age		0.014	0.012	0.010	0.008
		(0.015)	(0.015)	(0.020)	(0.020)
Ga		0.194	0.107	0.099	0.097
		(0.481)	(0.473)	(0.536)	(0.541)
Ewe		−0.253	−0.170	−0.198	−0.182
		(0.494)	(0.498)	(0.533)	(0.527)
Enumerator bias			−0.994*	−0.917*	−0.895*
			(0.413)	(0.448)	(0.444)
Cosmopolitanism					
Education				−0.106	−0.070
				(0.147)	(0.153)
Years in Accra				0.001	0.002
				(0.017)	(0.017)
Nigerian area				−0.124	−0.159
				(0.410)	(0.413)
Occupation					
Unemployed					0.377
					(0.872)
Trader					0.409
					(0.486)
Constant	−0.725***	−1.341*	−0.820	−0.480	−0.839
	(0.219)	(0.648)	(0.679)	(0.827)	(1.002)
Pseudo R^2	0.083	0.094	0.128	0.131	0.134
Observations	191	191	191	191	189

Robust standard errors in parentheses
Significance levels: ˆ$p \leq 0.10$; *$p \leq 0.05$; **$p \leq 0.01$; ***$p \leq 0.001$.

controls for whether or not the respondent was in a "Nigerian area" at the time the survey was administered.[8] Greater exposure

---

[8] Nigerian and non-Nigerian areas were categorized according to the neighborhoods the Nigerian enumerators selected when surveying Nigerian immigrants.

to Nigerian immigrants might either fuel or alleviate exclusionary attitudes.[9] Model (5) accounts for a respondent's occupation.[10]

Table 3.2 indicates that the single most substantive, significant, and robust determinant of exclusionary attitudes on the part of Ghanaian respondents is simply the immigrant group about which they were questioned. Holding all other variables at their mean or median, Ghanaians are 22 percent likely to vote for a Hausa but only 6 percent likely to vote for a Yoruba.[11] This difference is significant at the 99.9 percent confidence level, and it overwhelms every other potential determinant of exclusionary attitudes such as sex, age, ethnic identity, education, or occupation.[12]

Table 3.3 reproduces the same analysis for the respondent's own probability of voting for a Yoruba/Hausa presidential candidate. Table 3.3 further confirms the results from Table 3.2. Ghanaians are significantly less likely to vote for a Yoruba presidential candidate than they are to vote for a Hausa presidential candidate. This result is robust to a number of different specifications. Table 3.3 further indicates that male respondents tend to be less discriminating than female respondents, and that members of the Ewe ethnic group are more discriminating than are members of the dominant Akan ethnic group. In fact, Ewes are not only generally more discriminating than Akans; their

---

[9] There is a debate as to whether intergroup contact increases (Blalock 1967) or decreases (Allport 1954) intergroup hostility.

[10] The category *Student* was dropped because the two students in the sample responded "No," thus offering no variation in the outcome of interest.

[11] These estimates were calculated using *Clarify* (see Tomz et al. 2003; King et al. 2000) on Table 5, Model (5), excluding the dropped variable *Student*. Continuous controls were held at their mean. Binary controls were held at their median.

[12] Another model that includes interaction terms between *Yoruba* and all of the control variables enumerated in Table 2 was also tested. The only significant interaction term is the positive effect of the interaction between the *Yoruba* treatment variable and the enumerator variable, indicating that the female enumerator elicited less exclusionary responses toward Yorubas than did the male enumerator. The main *Yoruba* treatment variable remains, in all specifications, negative and statistically significant. No other interaction terms are significant, so the results are not presented here.

TABLE 3.3. *Probability of an Affirmative Answer to: "Would You Vote for a Yoruba/Hausa?"*

	Model (1)	Model (2)	Model (3)	Model (4)	Model (5)
Yoruba	−1.770***	−1.827***	−1.897***	−1.875***	−1.904***
	(0.452)	(0.450)	(0.488)	(0.496)	(0.511)
Demographic					
Sex		0.482	0.577	0.671	0.972^
		(0.407)	(0.406)	(0.420)	(0.540)
Age		0.022	0.020	0.010	0.006
		(0.016)	(0.015)	(0.020)	(0.021)
Ga		0.274	0.168	0.005	−0.083
		(0.499)	(0.494)	(0.576)	(0.582)
Ewe		−1.084^	−1.054^	−1.166^	−1.196^
		(0.607)	(0.614)	(0.677)	(0.686)
Enumerator bias			−1.327**	−1.272**	−1.243**
			(0.463)	(0.491)	(0.480)
Cosmopolitanism					
Education				−0.107	−0.040
				(0.167)	(0.176)
Years in Accra				0.011	0.018
				(0.018)	(0.019)
Nigerian area				−0.109	−0.225
				(0.441)	(0.449)
Occupation					
Unemployed					−0.798
					(0.904)
Trader					0.584
					(0.572)
Constant	−0.773***	−1.708**	−1.077	−0.662	−1.213
	(0.221)	(0.685)	(0.717)	(0.871)	(1.091)
Pseudo R^2	0.102	0.155	0.209	0.213	0.222
Observations	191	191	191	191	189

Robust standard errors in parentheses
Significance levels: ^$p \leq 0.10$; *$p \leq 0.05$; **$p \leq 0.01$; ***$p \leq 0.001$.

discrimination of Yorubas relative to Hausas is greater than the Akans'. Indeed, 0 percent of Ewe respondents would vote for a Yoruba, compared to 8 percent of Akan respondents. Furthermore, 17 percent of Ewe respondents would vote for a Hausa, compared to 33 percent of Akan respondents. The Ewe effect is equivalent to a 100 percent decrease in the likelihood of voting for a Yoruba versus a Hausa. In contrast, the Akan effect is equivalent to a 76 percent decrease in the likelihood of voting for a Yoruba versus a Hausa.[13]

This result is significant because Ewes constitute a minority group in Accra, which lost political power after Ghana's 2000 election and has historically experienced less economic advancement than the Akan.[14] Members of the Ewe ethnic group are thus more likely to feel threatened by immigrants' access to indigenous benefits.

The results so far indicate that Ghanaians hold more exclusionary attitudes toward Hausas than they do toward Yorubas. The identity of the immigrant group in question overwhelms any other potential determinant of exclusion: no matter what the Ghanaian's sex, age, ethnic identity, education level, or occupation, she is more likely to exclude a Yoruba than a Hausa.

A further test of the theory might look at Ghanaians' exclusionary attitudes toward Christian and Muslim Yorubas. Indeed, if cultural overlap determines which immigrant groups are threatening to host populations, then we should not expect Muslim Yorubas – who share as little overlap with Accra society as do Hausas – to represent a threat to Ghanaians in the capital, who would likely lump together all Muslims into one nonthreatening minority. The case of the 1969 Alien Compliance order, an expulsion decree that affected Ghana's aliens – and primarily its Yoruba population – provides an opportunity to test the observable implication of the argument for Christian versus Muslim Yorubas. On November 18, 1969, Prime Minister Busia of Ghana issued a Compliance Order, giving all aliens without valid documentation two weeks to leave the country. The move followed a number of decrees by the economic commissioner to restrict alien economic activity, and caused the departure of more than 100,000 foreigners (Peil 1979). The Alien Compliance

---

[13] A simpler way to illustrate this effect would be to add an interaction term between the *Yoruba* treatment variable and the *Ewe* binary variable. However, because all Ewes responded "No" to the question "Would you vote for a Yoruba?", this interaction term is automatically dropped from the model.

[14] See Minorities At Risk Project (2003).

Order, in its language, did not target any single group of aliens, but rather "aliens, both Africans and non-Africans in Ghana, [who] do not possess the requisite resident permits in conformity with the laws of Ghana" (Sudarkasa 1979). The Ghanaian government thus never codified formally into law or public rhetoric the discrimination of any one group. Indeed, a content analysis of Ghana's *Daily Graphic* newspaper and of the periodical *West Africa* in 1969 confirms that the government never explicitly singled out a group of aliens over others, and even claimed a number of times that "the laws were aimed at ensuring the security of the State and were not discriminatory against any national" (*Daily Graphic* 1969). Instead, scapegoating occurred informally, through pressure that Ghanaians and the Ghanaian police exerted on some groups over others.

The argument in this book implies that Yorubas, more than Hausas, should have been affected by this Alien Compliance Order. More specifically, it implies that Christian Yorubas, rather than Muslim Yorubas, should have been its victims. The survey of Yoruba and Hausa immigrants in Accra offers a test of the probability that an immigrant was affected by Ghana's 1969 mass immigrant expulsion, by measuring whether or not the immigrant responded "Yes" to the question "Did you or a family member have to leave Ghana because of the Alien Quit Order of 1969?"

Figure 3.2 indicates that the Yorubas sampled in Accra were much more affected than the sampled Hausas. These patterns confirm the exclusionary trends explored earlier. But even more to the point, there is an important difference in the proportion of Christian versus Muslim Yorubas who were affected by this mass immigrant expulsion: 55 percent of Christian Yorubas sampled were affected, compared to 40 percent of Muslim Yorubas sampled.

This measure of exclusion is less than perfect. It asks immigrants to self-report whether they were affected by an expulsion event that took place four decades earlier. Furthermore, it is drawn from the non-probability sample of immigrant groups: any result is thus difficult to generalize beyond the sampled respondents. Nevertheless, the empirical patterns explored here point to

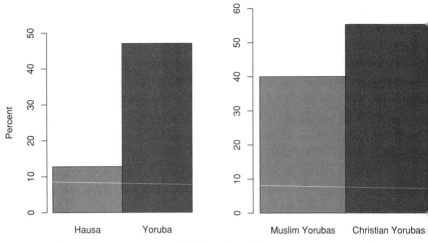

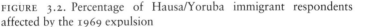

FIGURE 3.2. Percentage of Hausa/Yoruba immigrant respondents affected by the 1969 expulsion

a singular trend: the positive correlation between cultural overlap between immigrants and hosts and exclusion by hosts.

Qualitative evidence drawn from a set of structured interviews conducted with forty-three Yorubas in Ogbomosho, Nigeria, in June 2007 further complements this analysis. In these interviews, respondents were asked who, in their opinion, was affected by the Alien Compliance Order (ACO). Respondent answers to this question corroborate the finding that Yorubas were targeted over Hausas, and that Christian Yorubas were targeted over Muslim Yorubas. Table 3.4 summarizes these responses. It indicates a general consensus over the fact that Yorubas were targeted while Hausas were able to stay. It further shows a nontrivial number of respondents claiming that Muslim Yorubas were able to escape the fate of the ACO.[15]

---

[15] It is not unreasonable to doubt the validity of such claims given that they come largely from Christian Yorubas themselves. However, Christian Yorubas have no incentive to distort the truth today when recounting an event that occurred in 1969. Furthermore, given that close to half of all respondents actually claim that Muslim Yorubas were not necessarily able to stay during the ACO, there is reason to believe that these answers were not just a product of Christian Yorubas trying to attract sympathy.

TABLE 3.4. *The Targets of the 1969 Alien Compliance Order*

Question	Percentage
Who did the ACO target, if anyone? (open-ended)	
Aliens	16.28%
Nigerians	9.30%
Yorubas	48.84%
Don't Know	6.98%
Other	11.62%
Missing Data	6.98%
Were Hausas able to stay in Ghana during the ACO?	
Yes	74.42%
No	6.98%
Don't Know	9.30%
Missing Data	9.30%
Were Muslim Yorubas able to stay in Ghana during the ACO?	
Yes	23.26%
No	48.84%
Don't Know	6.98%
Missing Data	20.93%
	N = 43

Nigerien Exclusion of Yorubas and Hausas in Niamey

Which immigrant group do Nigeriens in Niamey exclude? Niamey presents the opposite setup to Accra. Indeed, it is the Hausas – not the Yorubas – who share cultural traits with their host society in Niamey. Not only are they Muslim; they are also Hausa. The Hausa immigrants in Niamey thus share both an ethnic and a religious identity with their hosts.

Figure 3.3 illustrates the difference in responses between Nigeriens who were asked about their attitudes of exclusion toward Yorubas and those who were asked about their attitudes of exclusion toward Kanawa Hausas. (Recall, from Chapter 1, that the ethnic label used for Hausas in Niamey is Kanawa.) It indicates a seven percentage-point difference between Nigeriens' beliefs that other Nigeriens would vote for a Yoruba (13%) and their beliefs that other Nigeriens would vote for a Kanawa Hausa (6%). This difference is significant at the 95 percent confidence

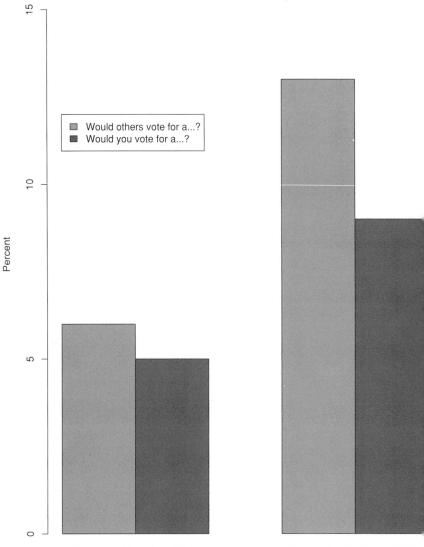

FIGURE 3.3. Exclusionary attitudes toward Yorubas and Hausas among Nigeriens in Niamey

TABLE 3.5. *Summary Statistics for Nigerien Respondents in Niamey*

	Kanawa Hausa Questionnaire		Yoruba Questionnaire	
	Mean	St. Deviation	Mean	St. Deviation
Sex (male=1)	0.48	0.50	0.39	0.49
Age	34.55	13.24	33.22	14.7
Zerma ethnicity	0.4	0.49	0.57	0.50
Tuareg ethnicity	0.02	0.14	0.02	0.14
Peul ethnicity	0.06	0.24	0.04	0.20
Hausa ethnicity	0.41	0.49	0.31	0.46
Enumerator	0.50	0.50	0.50	0.50
Years lived in Niamey	26.16	12.93	26.18	15.11
Nigerian area	0.50	0.50	0.50	0.50
Unemployed	0.03	0.17	0.01	0.10
Trader	0.51	0.50	0.42	0.50
Student	0.14	0.35	0.09	0.29
Observations	100		100	

level in a one-tailed test, and at the 90 percent confidence level in a two-tailed test. Furthermore, Nigerien respondents were more willing to vote for a Yoruba presidential candidate (9%) than for a Kanawa (5%), but this difference is not statistically significant at the conventional levels.

Table 3.5 provides summary statistics for the sample population responding to the Yoruba questionnaire and the sample population responding to the Kanawa questionnaire. The two samples are balanced on most characteristics, reflecting the randomization of the Yoruba versus Kanawa Hausa questionnaires; yet balance is not achieved among the Zerma respondents: 40 percent of respondents receiving the Kanawa Hausa questionnaire were Zerma, compared to 57 percent of respondents receiving the Yoruba questionnaire. This difference is statistically significant at the 95 percent confidence level in a two-tailed *t*-test.

In an effort to adjust for this imbalance, and to more precisely estimate the effect of receiving the Yoruba versus the Kanawa Hausa treatment, the following model is estimated:

$$ProbAffirmative_i = a + b_Y(Yoruba_i) + \mathbf{b_X X_i} + e_i \qquad (3.2)$$

where i is the Nigerien respondent, *ProbAffirmative* is the probability that a respondent answers "Yes" to the question "Do you believe Nigeriens would vote for a Yoruba (Kanawa)?", *Yoruba* is a dummy variable for whether the respondent received the Yoruba or Kanawa questionnaire, and **X** is a vector of control variables from Table 3.5.

In Table 3.6, Models (1) through (5) below estimate Equation (3.2). The independent variable of interest is *Yoruba*, a dummy variable that takes the value "1" if the respondent received the Yoruba questionnaire, and "0" if the respondent received the Kanawa questionnaire. The omitted category for the set of ethnic group variables is *Hausa*. A control for the *Tuareg* ethnic group was also incuded, but was dropped automatically because all four Tuaregs in the sample responded "No," offering no variation on the dependent variable. The results in Table 3.6 indicate that Kanawas evoke greater exclusion than Yorubas, even when we account for a Nigerien respondent's sex, age, ethnic identity, education level, and occupation. This result is robust to the inclusion and exclusion of a variety of controls. Table 3.6 further indicates that education has a significant and positive effect on the likelihood of voting for an ethnic other. Nigeriens with more education are more likely to exhibit inclusive attitudes toward ethnic others, perhaps because they are less likely to compete economically with urban immigrant traders. Finally, the enumerator effect is significant and thus controlled for here.

In sum, the results in Table 3.6 indicate that Nigeriens are more likely to express exclusionary attitudes toward Kanawas than they are toward Yorubas. In Niamey, where Islam and Hausa are indigenous identities, the host population exhibits a greater propensity to exclude immigrants who are both Muslim and Hausa.

3.3 Testing the Link between Cultural Overlap and Exclusion

The analysis so far shows that Ghanaians are more likely to exclude Yorubas than Hausas, and that Nigeriens are more likely

TABLE 3.6. *Probability of an Affirmative Answer to: "Do You Think Nigeriens Would Vote for a Yoruba/Kanawa?"*

	Model (1)	Model (2)	Model (3)	Model (4)	Model (5)
Yoruba	0.851^	0.918^	0.994*	1.157*	1.205*
	(0.517)	(0.508)	(0.504)	(0.523)	(0.582)
Demographic					
Sex		0.815^	0.757	0.687	0.699
		(0.490)	(0.517)	(0.563)	(0.541)
Age		−0.001	0.003	0.015	0.012
		(0.016)	(0.016)	(0.026)	(0.026)
Zerma		0.123	0.019	0.264	0.233
		(0.479)	(0.502)	(0.544)	(0.565)
Peul		0.010	−0.629	−0.103	−0.163
		(1.213)	(1.228)	(1.194)	(1.368)
Enumerator bias			0.634**	0.599*	0.587*
			(0.219)	(0.244)	(0.244)
Cosmopolitanism					
Education				0.259^	0.299^
				(0.157)	(0.170)
Years in Niamey				−0.010	−0.006
				(0.029)	(0.027)
Nigerian area				0.181	0.181
				(0.624)	(0.638)
Occupation					
Unemployed					1.366
					(1.291)
Trader					−0.514
					(0.663)
Student					−0.026
					(0.905)
Constant	−2.751***	−3.186***	−5.159***	−6.136***	−6.051**
	(0.422)	(0.603)	(1.023)	(1.221)	(1.426)
Pseudo R^2	0.023	0.045	0.134	0.142	0.158
Observations	200	196	196	191	190

Robust standard errors in parentheses
Significance levels: ^$p \leq 0.10$; *$p \leq 0.05$; **$p \leq 0.01$; ***$p \leq 0.001$.

to exclude Kanawa Hausas than Yorubas. But how do we know that this is so because of the threat that cultural overlap poses to the indigenous population? To hone in on the mechanism, this section surveys four alternative explanations for why Ghanaians might exclude Yorubas and Nigeriens might exclude Hausas, and shows that the data do not support these alternative stories.

A prevalent explanation of ethnic violence is Chua's (2004) analysis of the backlash economically successful ethnic minorities tend to experience. In her book *World on Fire*, Amy Chua points out unsettling patterns of violence against economically successful ethnic minorities in countries that simultaneously introduce economic capitalism and political liberalization (Chua 2004). She echoes the economic threat literature on immigrant exclusion, and thus raises the question: Are Yorubas more excluded than Hausas in Accra because they are better-off? Are Hausas more excluded than Yorubas in Niamey because they are wealthier? The economic success of Yorubas and Hausas in Ghana and Niger, in fact, does not explain the patterns of rejection and acceptance described in the previous section, for two reasons. Immigrant survey data on Yorubas and Hausas in Accra and in Niamey indicates that sampled Yorubas are wealthier than sampled Hausas in Accra *and* in Niamey. In Accra, 72 percent of sampled Yorubas live in houses with cement walls, whereas only 50 percent of sampled Hausas live in houses with cement walls; conversely, whereas only 5 precent of sampled Yorubas live in houses with mud walls, 18 percent of sampled Hausas live in houses with mud walls. In Niamey, 40 percent of sampled Yorubas live in houses with cement walls whereas 33 percent of sampled Hausas live in houses with cement walls; conversely, 59 percent of sampled Yorubas live in houses with mud walls whereas as many as 67 percent of sampled Hausas live in houses with mud walls.[16] Figure 3.4 illustrates these patterns. The data from the sample of Nigerian immigrants in Niamey indicate that Yorubas are better off than Hausas in both Accra and in Niamey.

---

[16] Incomes in the developing world tend to be more erratic than are incomes in industrialized countries. This makes it difficult for respondents to answer a question that presupposes a regular source of income. Furthermore, this means that consumption-related expenditures, such as housing quality, are a more reliable indicator of longer-term economic well-being (Banerjee and Duflo 2007; Deaton 1998). Here, cement walls indicate greater wealth than mud walls.

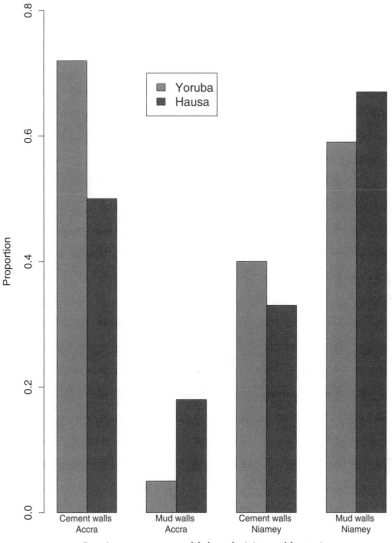

FIGURE 3.4. Immigrant group wealth by ethnicity and host city

Economic well-being, therefore, cannot account for the differences found across cities.

A second explanation focuses on demographic factors (Quillian 1995; Posner 2004b) and migration waves (Olzak

1989). A group becomes threatening, or salient, by virtue of its size or recent arrival. The demographic explanation would argue that Yorubas are less accepted than Hausas in Accra because they form a bigger demographic entity; similarly, Kanawa Hausas are less accepted than Yorubas in Niamey because they are the larger group. According to this argument, Accra Yorubas and Kanawa Hausas in Niamey are more threatening because, owing to their size, they represent greater competition for scarce resources (Quillian 1995) or they can be mobilized by political entrepreneurs (Quillian 1995; Posner 2004b). Actual demographic data do not exist for immigrant populations by ethnicity in Ghana and in Niger; it is therefore difficult to assess the veracity of these claims. Two pieces of evidence from the field, however, suggest that demographics cannot explain the variation in Yoruba and Hausa exclusion in Accra and in Niamey. First, interviews with Nigerian community leaders in Niamey indicate that Yorubas, not Hausas, are the larger immigrant group in Niamey.[17] Second, host society respondents rarely mention demographic factors when they are asked to identify characteristics of each immigrant group. Only 3 percent of host respondents in Niamey cited population size as a differentiating characteristic of Yorubas in Niamey; none cited population size as a differentiating characteristic of Kanawa Hausas in Niamey.[18]

A related explanation would argue that Yorubas in Accra are more recent migrants than Hausas in Accra and that Kanawa Hausas in Niamey are more recent migrants than Yorubas in Niamey. According to this argument, host societies perceive these groups as more threatening because of their recent influx. Evidence from immigrant surveys in the field, however, suggests

---

[17] Interview with the secretary general of the Nigerian Community Union in Niamey, Niger (a member of the Igbo ethnic group): February 28, 2007.

[18] Shack and Skinner (1979) echo this insight that demographic factors seem not to matter in determining immigrant exclusion in Africa: "There would appear to be no direct correlation between the demographic ratio of strangers to hosts, on the one hand, and the territorial size of the host society, on the other, in determining a society's capacity to accommodate strangers within its political boundaries" (Shack and Skinner 1979: 14).

that both Yorubas and Hausas have settled in Accra since the late nineteenth century. In Niamey, the survey of Yoruba and Hausa immigrants indicates that Yorubas migrated beginning in the late 1930s, whereas Hausas migrated beginning in the early 1960s. Migration waves, therefore, could contribute to the exclusion patterns we witness in Niamey, but they cannot explain the migration patterns we witness in Accra.

A third explanation would predict that groups with more naturalized citizens are better integrated. Immigrant survey data indicate that more Hausas in Accra indeed have Ghanaian passports than do Yorubas in Accra (68% versus 47%). However, only 10 percent of Nigerian Yorubas sampled in Niamey – compared to 20 percent of Nigerian Hausas sampled – have Nigerien passports. Naturalization, therefore, cannot explain why Yorubas are better integrated than Hausas in Niamey. Furthermore, given the analysis in Chapter 2, naturalization may be endogenous to immigrants' decisions to signal in-group attachment to their leaders. In this case, naturalization cannot be used as an exogenous factor explaining immigrant integration: immigrants choose to naturalize, and host societies can choose to make such a process easy or difficult for the applicant.[19]

A final alternative explanation for the varying acceptance and rejection of Yorubas and Hausas in Ghana and in Niger goes back to the differentiated roles that various ethnic groups played under colonial rule. Colonial powers used nonindigenous African populations as intermediaries: the historical role these nonindigenous minorities may have played in their respective host countries could contribute to host exclusion today. For example, the Beninois became easy scapegoats and were expelled throughout West Africa because of the special attention they received from the French. Challenor (1979) explains that the French placed the relatively well-educated Beninois (then Dahomeyans) into colonial bureaucracies throughout West Africa and that, once

---

[19] The chief of the Yoruba Community in Niamey, Niger, explains that "if you naturalize, then it's assumed you don't go back to your country." Interview by the author, Niamey, Niger: September 27, 2007.

TABLE 3.7. *Summarizing and Evaluating Alternative Hypotheses*

Hypothesis	Explains Exclusion in Accra?	Explains Exclusion in Niamey?
Economic wealth	Yes	No
Demographic size	Not tested	No
Migration timing	No	Yes
Naturalization	Yes	No
Colonial legacy	No	No

independent, nations such as Côte d'Ivoire and Niger expelled all their Beninois immigrants in reaction to this imposition (Challenor 1979). Did the Yoruba play a particularly antagonistic role in the history of Ghana? Similarly, did Nigerian Hausas impose themselves in Niger?

The British indeed used colonial subjects to help stave off the Ashanti incursions into the land of the Gas in the nineteenth century.[20] However, the British relied primarily on Hausas, not Yorubas, to fight the Ashanti wars, meaning that the exclusion of Yorubas in Accra cannot stem from this colonial legacy (Gomda 2006). Finally, Niger was a French colony, and Nigeria a British colony: Yorubas and Hausas were thus equally unlikely to interact with Nigerien society through the colonial system. There is thus no empirical evidence supporting the claim that relations between Ghanaians and Yorubas on one hand, and Nigeriens and Nigerian Hausas on the other, are a product of antagonistic relations shaped by colonial powers.

Table 3.7 summarizes the alternative hypotheses surveyed in this section, and how well they elucidate the patterns of exclusion uncovered in this chapter. It reveals that these alternative explanations work, at best, on patterns of exclusion in one city, but they cannot explain exclusion across the two localities.

---

[20] The Anglo-Asante wars of the nineteenth century refer to conflicts between the Asante (Ashanti) Empire in the interior part of what is today known as Ghana, and the British colonial empire in the Gold Coast. The Fante and Ga coastal people relied on the British Empire to fight off the Ashanti incursions.

3.4 Conclusion

This chapter has argued that cultural similarities can exacerbate immigrant-host relations because they threaten indigenous hosts trying to protect and limit access to indigenous resources. Data analysis from surveys of host populations in Accra and Niamey provide empirical evidence for the implication that cultural overlap increases exclusion. In Accra, Yorubas share religious similarities with Ghanaians while Hausas, who are overwhelmingly Muslim, are culturally distinct. Yet Ghanaians in Accra exclude Yorubas significantly more than they do Hausas. In Niamey, Nigerian Hausas share a wide cultural repertoire with indigenous Nigeriens, through both a shared ethnicity (Hausa) and a shared religion (Muslim). Yet Nigeriens in Niamey exclude Kanawa Hausas more than they do Yorubas. Finally, the religious split among the Yorubas of Accra allows for an additional controlled comparison of exclusion based on cultural overlap. The evidence shows that Christian Yorubas, who share a larger cultural repertoire with Christian Accra than do Muslim Yorubas, face higher levels of exclusion from their host society.

But a number of questions remain. The collection of survey data runs into potential complications, from internal validity to external validity, and certainly precludes us from making causal claims. In an effort to offer a more compelling story, the empirical analysis does not stop here. In the following chapter I consider in greater depth a number of alternative explanations for the patterns of exclusion against Yorubas and Hausas. In so doing, I show that the argument put forth in this book is most consistent with the patterns uncovered in the data.

4

Alternative Explanations

The evidence used in this book to substantiate the claim that cultural overlap may yield greater exclusion among immigrant minorities in urban West Africa is drawn from several sources of data. Interview data with Yoruba, Hausa, and indigenous members of Accra, Cotonou, and Niamey provide qualitative evidence linking cultural overlap to the threat of group identity loss and to greater immigrant group attachment. Survey data with Yoruba and Hausa immigrants in Accra, Cotonou and Niamey provide quantitative evidence linking cultural overlap to greater immigrant group attachment. Survey data with indigenous members of Accra and Niamey provide quantitative statistical evidence linking cultural overlap to greater host exclusion. These diverse sources of data are woven together in this book to substantiate a counterintuitive claim that cultural similarities can exacerbate immigrant exclusion.

In this chapter I provide additional evidence for the argument, tackling questions of internal and external validity that are characteristic of largely observational data. First, I demonstrate the robustness of my findings. Second, I dispel concerns about potential confounding effects. Finally, I tackle other methodological issues specific to the use of survey instruments.

4.1 Robustness Test

Chapter 3 articulates and tests the link between cultural overlap and exclusion by hosts. It argues that cultural overlap between immigrants and hosts increases political exclusion of immigrants by hosts. It posits that this is so because cultural overlap increases the threat of immigrant assimilation and access to indigenous resources and benefits.

An additional way of capturing this counterintuitive claim is to systematically analyze host respondents' qualitative answers to the open-ended question: "What, if anything, differentiates Yorubas/Hausas from Ghanaians (Nigeriens)?"[1] This question allowed host respondents to elaborate on the characteristics they believe make the nonindigenous ethnic group in question different from themselves. In this part of the survey, a nontrivial proportion of respondents explicitly claimed that nothing differentiates them from the ethnic group in question. The respondent's propensity to make such an explicit claim can be seen here as an indicator of the respondent's effort (or not) to raise barriers between herself and the immigrant group in question. It is reasonable to interpret the information in that manner because of the order in which questions were asked in the survey. This open-ended question came *after* the voting questions that measure political exclusion by hosts. In other words, after priming the respondent to think about political competition, she is asked to identify and voice the differentiating characteristics between herself and Yorubas or Hausas. Who do host respondents exclude once they are primed to think about competition over political resources?

Figure 4.1 indicates what proportion of Ghanaians and Nigeriens expressed no differences between themselves and Yorubas (Hausas). It illustrates a pattern that is consistent with the empirical analysis in Chapter 3, that hosts are more likely to raise barriers between themselves and high-overlap immigrant

---

[1] This question, like the voting questions, is drawn from Posner (2004b).

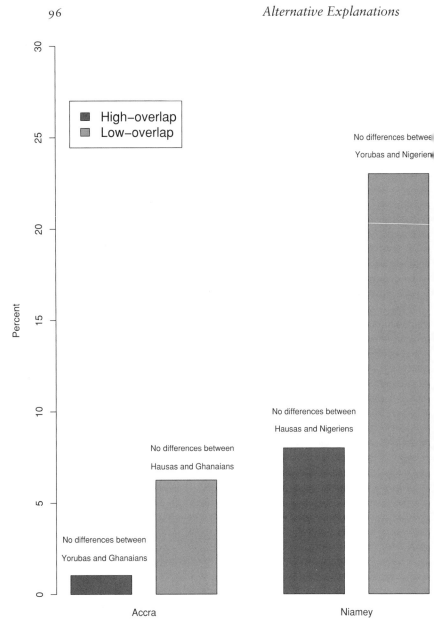

FIGURE 4.1. Proportion of indigenous respondents who expressed no differences with Yorubas/Hausas

groups. In this figure, they are less likely to say that nothing differentiates them from the high-overlap group than they are to say that nothing differentiates them from the low-overlap group. In the typical regression models estimated in Chapter 3 (not shown here), these effects are statistically significant at least at the 90 percent confidence level for the Ghanaian case and at least at the 95 percent confidence level for the Nigerien case. These tests provide additional evidence for the argument by showing how indigenous hosts explicitly create cultural barriers between themselves and high-overlap immigrant groups once they are primed to think about political competition.

4.2 Confounding Effects

Selection Bias

This book looks at communities of voluntary migrants. Because migration is voluntary, a possible selection bias exists in the types of people who choose to migrate to a certain location. Say there are two types of migrants, a "sociable" migrant and a "nonsociable" migrant. If sociable Yorubas and nonsociable Hausas are more likely to migrate to Niamey, while nonsociable Yorubas and sociable Hausas are more likely to migrate to Accra, we would observe the same patterns presented here, but for reasons unrelated to cultural overlap and resistance to assimilation. How can we be sure that the patterns of exclusion we find in the data are not attributable to a selection bias in the types of migrant communities who choose to settle in various locations?

There is a theoretical and an empirical response to this objection. First, it is unclear ex ante in which direction this bias might tilt. For example, nonsociable migrants are more likely to want to settle in localities where they share little cultural overlap with their hosts. Conversely, sociable migrants are more likely to want to settle in localities where they share cultural traits with their hosts. In this case, nonsociable migrants are more likely to be low-overlap groups while sociable migrants are more likely to be high-overlap groups. Yet the findings indicate that low-overlap groups (nonsociable migrants in this scenario) are less excluded than high-overlap groups (sociable migrants in this scenario). There is thus no reason to believe that the excluded group is simply a less sociable one; more generally, there is no reason to believe that the self-selection of immigrants systematically creates the exclusionary outcomes observed in Accra and Niamey.

Empirically, it is possible to cast further doubt on selection bias by showing that Yorubas who go to Accra are not that different of a community from those who go to Niamey. Similarly, if Hausas who settle in Accra are similar to Hausas who settle in Niamey, we can dispel the hypothesis that different types of Hausas settle in different places. I therefore test whether Yorubas and Hausas self-select into similar or different networks in Accra and Niamey. Namely, if Yorubas and Hausas are different "types" of communities in different cities, we might expect to find them self-selecting into different types of occupational networks in the two localities. Figures 4.2 and 4.3 illustrate the distribution of occupations of Hausa and Yoruba respondents in Accra and Niamey. Figure 4.2 compares the occupations of Yorubas in Accra and Niamey. Figure 4.3 compares the occupations of Hausas in Accra and Niamey.

Figures 4.2 and 4.3 show strikingly similar distributions of occupations for both groups in the two localities. Yorubas in both Accra and Niamey are primarily traders and electricians. Although a slightly greater proportion of Yorubas in Accra are students and unemployed relative to Yorubas in Niamey, the Yoruba community largely settles as traders, electricians, tailors, and barbers in both localities. The similarity in occupation between Hausas in Accra and Hausas in Niamey is even more striking. In both localities, Hausas are primarily traders and tailors. A number of them are unemployed, but this holds true in both cities. If different types of Hausas and Yorubas selected into different host cities, subsequently explaining varying exclusion outcomes, we would expect to see strikingly different economic networks for these communities in each locality. The data indicate, however, that Hausas and Yorubas self-select into very similar networks between Accra and Niamey. This evidence casts doubt on the self-selection hypothesis.

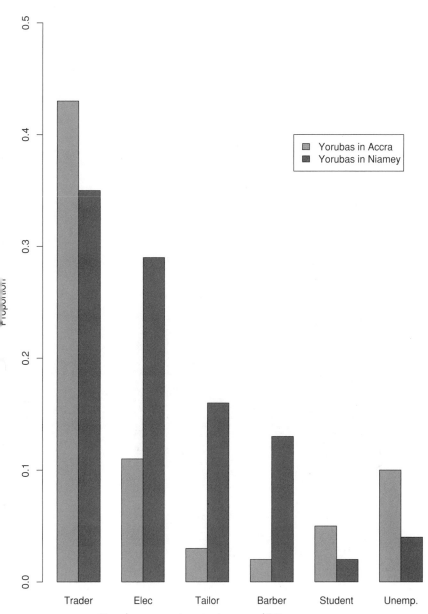

FIGURE 4.2. Yoruba occupations in Accra and Niamey

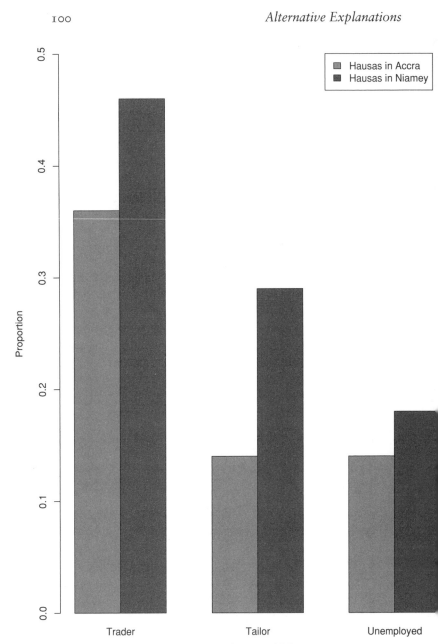

FIGURE 4.3. Hausa occupations in Accra and Niamey

Geography

An alternative confounding story for the varying degrees of immigrant attachment to the host community is geographical. Figure 4.4 illustrates the approximate location of each ethnic group's homeland (in bold): Yorubaland is closer to Ghana than is Hausaland. Conversely, Hausaland is closer to Niger than is Yorubaland.[2] Could Yorubas in Accra be tighter-knit than Hausas simply because of their proximity to their homeland? Could Hausas in Niamey be more attached to their immigrant community because Hausaland extends from northern Nigeria into Niger, whereas Yorubaland is farther from Niger's capital?

Four factors cast doubt on this geographical argument. First, on a theoretical level, one could imagine geographical proximity having either a positive or a negative effect on immigrant group attachment in a host city. On one hand, groups that are geographically closer to their homelands face lower costs to maintaining physical and financial links with their hometowns. On the other hand, groups that are geographically farther from their homelands face greater incentives to organize within their host society precisely to counter the effect of distance. Geographical proximity, therefore, could have either a tightening or loosening effect on immigrant organization.

Second, the comparison of Christian and Muslim Yorubas in Accra offers a useful empirical case for testing this hypothesis. Christian and Muslim Yorubas are both from Yorubaland. Yet Chapter 2 clearly demonstrates diverging patterns of immigrant group attachment between Christian and Muslim Yorubas in Accra. To be fair, Muslim Yorubas may come from a different part of Yorubaland than do Christian Yorubas. Table 4.1 summarizes the major birth cities of Christian and Muslim Yorubas surveyed in Accra and born in Nigeria. It confirms that Muslim Yorubas tend to be born in cities that are farther from Accra than Christian Yorubas. Indeed, two-thirds of Muslim

---

[2] Figure 4.4 is a sketch and thus only approximates the locations of some historical ethnic homelands. It is by no means a comprehensive or a detailed map of all ethnic homelands in West Africa.

FIGURE 4.4. Ethnic homelands and nation-states in West Africa

TABLE 4.1. *Distance between Christian and Muslim Yoruba Hometowns and Accra*

Birth City	Christian Yorubas (Born in Nigeria)	Muslim Yorubas (Born in Nigeria)	Distance from Accra (Calculated Using Google Maps)
Ilorin	0%	25%	745 km; 10 h. 12 min.
Shaki	0%	12.5%	709 km; 9 h. 44 min.
Ogbomosho	27.5%	25%	692 km; 9 h. 28 min.
Ejigbo	5%	0%	670 km; 9 h. 25 min.
Ibadan	5%	12.5%	587 km; 8 h. 1 min.
Lagos	27.5%	0%	463 km; 6 h. 20 min.
N	40	8	

Yorubas – compared to just one-third of Christian Yorubas – must undertake a ten-to eleven-hour trip to go home. However, Table 4.1 also reveals that the range of variation among Yoruba birth cities is not wide: the shortest trip is six and a half hours long, compared to just over ten hours long for the longest trip. We should be skeptical of attributing differences in immigrant attachment to a three- to four-hour difference in a trip back home.[3]

A third test of this alternative claim is possible by looking at the breakdown, by Hausa hometown, of the Hausa community's attachment to its immigrant organization in Niamey. Most Nigerian Hausas in Niamey are born in Nigeria (70%) and they distribute themselves roughly into three home states. Approximately 48 percent of Nigerian Hausas surveyed are from Sokoto State, 24 percent are from Kebbi State and 24 percent are from Kaduna State. Table 4.2 compares the distance between each home state and Niamey, with the average in-group attachment scores for each Hausa subcommunity. As Table 4.2 and Figure 4.5 illustrate, there is no correlation between geographic distance from Niamey and in-group attachment. Hausas from Kaduna, which

---

[3] Note also that this analysis relies on the birthplace of Yorubas born in Nigeria, and thus on a very small number of observations: forty Christian Yorubas and eight Muslim Yorubas.

TABLE 4.2. *Distance from Niamey and In-Group Attachment*

Home State	Proportion of Hausas	Dist. from Niamey (Using Google Maps)	In-Group Attachment
Kaduna	24%	896 km; 12 h. 11 min.	0.51
Sokoto	48%	512 km; 6 h. 32 min.	0.40
Kebbi	24%	350 km; 5 h. 6 min.	0.33
N	21		

is farthest from Niamey, are most attached to their immigrant community.

Fourth, the analysis of in-group attachment levels among Yorubas and Hausas in Accra, Cotonou, and Niamey may be repeated excluding variables that are clearly a function of geography, namely (1) the proportion of respondents who traveled back to Nigeria in the past month, (2) the proportion of respondents whose children have schooled only in Nigeria, and (3) the proportion of respondents who send remittances home regularly.[4] Figure 4.6 illustrates patterns of in-group attachment when we exclude these measures. It indicates that the patterns continue to hold without these geographical variables.

This section has considered the possible confounding effects of immigrant self-selection and geography. First, I have tackled the argument that immigrants might self-select into different localities, demonstrating empirically that the occupational networks of Yorubas in Accra and Niamey, and of Hausas in Accra and Niamey, are similar. Second, I have considered the role that geography might play in explaining immigrant attachment to the immigrant community, and shown that there is no systematic correlation between distance from home and immigrant

---

[4] I do not count (1) the proportion of respondents who voted in the last Nigerian presidential elections, or (2) the proportion of respondents with a Nigerian passport, as variables that vary with geography because: (1) one need only travel to the border and be in Nigeria to vote, and (2) a passport is not needed to travel across ECOWAS countries, meaning that obtaining a passport is indicative of something more than just the desire to travel back home. I include remittances as a geography-dependent measure because these populations do not use formal institutions to send remittances home: they use instead informal means, which require personal trips or sending a trusted intermediary.

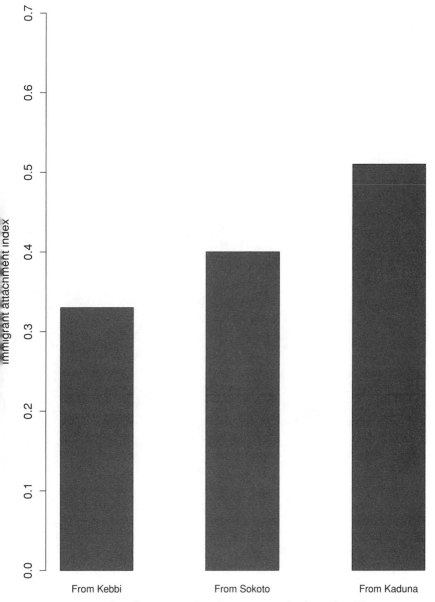

FIGURE 4.5. Attachment to immigrant organization, by Hausa hometown

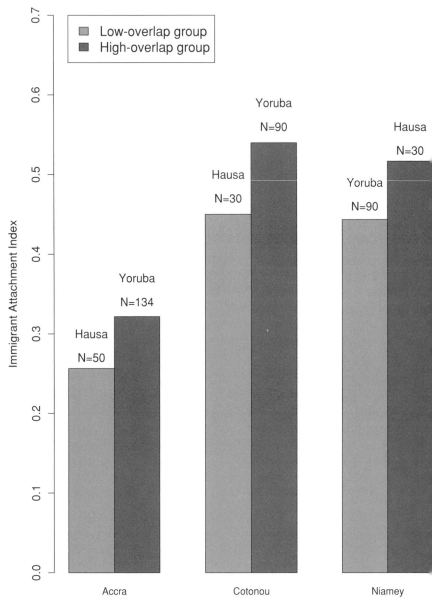

FIGURE 4.6. In-group attachment, excluding geographic variables

attachment levels. These additional analyses further lend credence to the argument that the immigrant attachment and exclusionary patterns we observe are due to cultural overlap.

4.3 The Term "Hausa" and Survey Validity

A different empirical concern stems from the ambiguous understanding of the term "Hausa" in Ghana. In Ghana, some have come to equate *Hausa* with *Muslim*. How does the analysis here ensure that survey respondents had the appropriate understanding of the term *Hausa* when asked whether they would vote for a Hausa? If the survey question does not capture the concept it is trying to measure, it lacks validity and cannot adequately inform us.

The term *Hausa* in Ghana has acquired a more fluid meaning to Ghanaians over time. I argue that this is not problematic, but instead indicative of Hausa integration into Ghanaian society through the Muslim minority. Still, I address the concern through four steps. First, I situate the Muslim community in Accra. In this section, I present the tension between religious and ethnic affiliations, which has characterized the Muslim community in Accra since its creation in the late nineteenth century. By doing so, I demonstrate that ethnic loyalties have always been and continue to be vibrant among Accra's Muslims, even though Islam acts as a glue that binds Muslim groups together, especially in the eyes of non-Muslims. Second, I argue and show that the ambiguous meaning of the term *Hausa* evolved over time precisely as a consequence of Hausa integration into a Muslim minority. In other words, I aim to show that it was precisely the absence of cultural overlap between Hausas and Ghanaian coastal society that allowed for the transformation of the term *Hausa* from one that designates an alien ethnic group to one that refers to a religious community. Third, I use interview sources to demonstrate that, while the debate over the meaning of the term Hausa does exist to some extent, common and public knowledge of Hausas' Nigerian origins is wide. Fourth, I show that my main results in the analysis of Ghanaian exclusion of Hausas and Yorubas in Accra continue to hold even when we restrict the sample to Ghanaians least likely to confuse *Hausa* with *Muslim*.

Scholars who have studied Accra's Muslim community have identified a gap between the semblance of unity and homogeneity from the outside and the reality of ethnic and national competition within. Jean Rouch, the French anthropologist and filmmaker, was one of the first to write, in 1956, about West African immigration into Ghana, then known as the Gold Coast. In his article "Migrations au Ghana," Rouch explains that while the Muslim community of the Gold Coast might seem like the natural identity cleavage, ethnic and national divisions and affiliations remain strong within this alien Muslim community (Rouch 1956: 170). In her 1985 article, "Muslim Segmentation: Cohesion and Divisiveness in Accra," Deborah Pellow surveys the evolving affiliations of Accra's Muslims over time, as groups fought over the location and leadership of Accra's Central Mosque: "Since the affiliative behaviour of these foreigners was situationally defined, under certain circumstances their Muslimness lost its salience and the far more exclusive identity of ethnicity was assumed" (Pellow 1985: 428). These scholars contrast the reality of the group's heterogeneity with its monolithic appearance to outsiders. In a way, they have identified an equilibrium, whereby "the validation of separate tribal heads, or identification with the ethnic group segment, neither necessitates nor creates disjunctions" (Pellow 1985: 428).

At the root of this characteristic balance between religious and ethnic identification is the fact that Islam was imported into Accra by West African immigrants. Jean Rouch notes that:

Islam was brought over entirely by emigrants into Gold Coast. It seems, therefore, that the Muslim community of the Gold Coast represents a more natural grouping than do ethnic or national ones. In fact, that is not at all the case.[5]

---

[5] "L'Islam est apporté entièrement par les émigrants en Gold Coast. Il semble donc que la communauté musulmane de Gold Coast représente un bloc plus naturel que les blocs ethniques ou nationaux. En fait, il n'en est rien" (Rouch 1956: 170). Translated from the French by the author.

Deborah Pellow echoes this claim:

Accra is a plural society made up of diverse collectivities, one of which is the Muslim community. The latter, in turn, was established, and is currently dominated, by migrant ethnic groups – primarily from Nigeria, as well as parts of French West Africa.[6]

This importation of Islam into Accra society means that, while Hausas arrived primarily as migrant traders, Islam eventually became a defining identity:

The collectivity represented a socio-religious as well as a spatial unity, and in opposition to their southern hosts, the Muslims carried greater salience than their respective hometown or ethnic origins. ... The Central Accra chiefs "moved together": Yoruba and Hausa shared the same *sarkin yaki* (captain of war), symbolic of the fact that these men would never go to war against one another.[7]

Yet originally, this association between Islam and migrant traders implied that the Muslim community in Accra came to be perceived as largely immigrant, suggesting that *Muslim* was first associated with *alien*:

The fact is that despite the growing number of Ghanaian converts, in the 1950s and today, Accra's Muslim community is largely immigrant in character, to the extent that Hausa, a foreign language, continues to serve as the lingua franca and is commonly the medium of instruction in Accra's Koranic schools.[8]

As Islam became a glue bringing together a variety of immigrant ethnic traders in Accra Hausa became the lingua franca for this community, reflecting the cohesiveness of a minority, who

looked and dressed alike, [and they] lived together at Zongo Lane and at Okanshie and Horse Road. ... They spoke little of the local language, communicating among themselves in Hausa; they sent their children to the same *makaranta* (Koranic school); and they married off their daughters to one another.[9]

[6] See Pellow (1985): 419.
[7] See Pellow (1985): 427.
[8] See Pellow (1985): 429.
[9] See Pellow (1985): 427.

It is within this context that the ambiguousness of the term *Hausa* emerged. As the language of communication among immigrant Muslims, *Hausa* came to be associated with the *alien* and the *Muslim*. Over time, however, the *Muslim* has eclipsed the *alien*. This trend came through in my interviews with members of the Hausa, Yoruba and indigenous communities in Accra. One Muslim Chief describes this confusion as follows: "Nigerians, Malians, etc... because they are all Muslims, they call themselves Hausa. But there are original Hausa people who are from Nigeria – but all Muslims refer to themselves as Hausas."[10] A Nigerian concurs, adding that the term Hausa now extends to indigenous Ghanaian ethnic groups as well: "Ghanaian northerners say they are Hausa because Hausa is a Muslim language."[11] When asked explicitly if there exists such a thing as a Ghanaian Hausa, one-third of Nigerians affected by Ghana's 1969 mass immigrant expulsion, interviewed in their hometown of Ogbomosho, Nigeria, in June 2007, answered positively.

Yet the opposite view was also widely expressed. A Nigerian Hausa explained that "It's not true that all Muslims are called Hausas. Nima is a Muslim place, not a Hausa place. There are many tribes that are not Hausa but are Muslim: Dagombas, Sassala."[12] One Christian Yoruba claims that "Hausas in Ghana are from Nigeria."[13] A Muslim Yoruba agrees: "If somebody tells you he's a Hausa and he's a Ghanaian, he's a liar. There's no Hausas in Ghana: they are Nigerians."[14] The ambiguousness is so prevalent that some respondents contradicted themselves during their interview:

In Ghana here, you have something they call Hausa tribe. So the moment you speak the language here, they can't differentiate you from somebody from outside... Here they don't have Hausa tribe but most of the people do speak the language... The original Hausas are not from Ghana.[15]

---

[10] Interview, Accra, Ghana: January 28(B), 2007.
[11] Interview, Accra, Ghana: January 22(C), 2007.
[12] Interview, Accra, Ghana: January 29(B), 2007.
[13] Interview, Accra, Ghana: February 6(A), 2007.
[14] Interview, Accra, Ghana: February 7(A), 2007.
[15] Interview, Accra, Ghana: February 5(A), 2007.

The confusion that transpires in this qualitative evidence follows naturally from the way in which Hausa migrants settled in Accra as importers of Islam. Since Islam did not previously exist in Accra society, the fact that it came to define Hausa migrants so fundamentally created no threat of assimilation for Hausas in the Gold Coast. Hausa leaders had thus no reason to resist this identification of *Hausa* with *Muslim*. As a result, the equation of Hausa with Muslim was unproblematic to both Hausa leaders and to the indigenous non-Muslim Ghanaians. Over time, this actually facilitated the integration of Hausas into Ghanaian coastal society such that, today, the Hausa language is increasingly considered to be a native Ghanaian language and the Hausas an indigenous Ghanaian ethnic group.

So far, I have argued that the ambiguousness of the *Hausa* term in southern Ghana is indicative of Hausa integration through its association with a non-threatening Muslim minority. I now turn to the empirical analysis of Ghanaian exclusion of Hausas and Yorubas in Accra and test whether the patterns of exclusion hold when we restrict the sample to Ghanaians who are less likely to conflate *Hausa* with *Muslim*. In other words, when we restrict the sample to individuals who interpret *Hausa* more strictly as an ethnic group rather than a religious identity, do these individuals continue to exclude Hausas less than they exclude Yorubas?

I offer two tests to shed light on this question. First, I compare the exclusion of Yorubas and Hausas in Accra when looking solely at Ghanaians who did not list Hausa as an indigenous Ghanaian language when asked to enumerate five native Ghanaian languages. Second, I repeat the analysis excluding a subsample of Ghanaians who explicitly state *only* religion as a differentiating characteristic of Hausas and Ghanaians. The idea behind these analyses is that they are harder tests because they exclude those most likely to equate *Hausa* with *Muslim*. Ghanaians who list *Hausa* as an indigenous Ghanaian language are more likely to also believe that indigenous Ghanaian Hausas, that is, Muslims, exist. Furthermore, Ghanaians who cite religion as the *only* difference between Hausas and Ghanaians are most likely to equate *Hausa* with *Muslim*.

The April 2007 survey of 200 indigenous Ghanaians asked primarily about Ghanaians' willingness to vote for a Yoruba or a Hausa. Each respondent was also first asked to list five indigenous Ghanaian languages. Approximately 43 percent of the sample included Hausa in that list, indicating the prevalence of beliefs about the indigenousness of Hausa as a Ghanaian language. This subsample of Ghanaians is also more likely to conflate the term *Hausa* with *Muslim*, because the Hausa language is the lingua franca among Accra's Muslims. A harder test of exclusionary behavior among Ghanaians might therefore exclude this subsample of Ghanaians, in an effort to "clean" the sample of any confusion with regard to the term "Hausa." Table 4.3 below provides results from a logit estimation of respondents' likelihood to vote for a Yoruba or a Hausa on such a subsample. It indicates that, even among those Ghanaians who did not list Hausa as an indigenous Ghanaian language, Yorubas are substantively and significantly more excluded than are Hausas.

A second test examines the weight of those respondents who explicitly and only cited religious differences between Hausas and Ghanaians when asked the question: "What, if anything, makes Yorubas (Hausas) different from Ghanaians?" One might argue that those Ghanaians who cited only religious differences are also more likely to associate the ethnic group with simply a religious identity. If this is the case, such respondents might be driving the result that Hausas are less excluded than Yorubas. The analysis yields four interesting findings.

First, while not a single respondent who received the Yoruba questionnaire cited only religious differences between Ghanaians and Yorubas, approximately 6.25 percent of respondents who received the Hausa questionnaire cited religious differences only between Ghanaians and Hausas. This is unsurprising, given that Accra is largely Christian, that Hausas are largely Muslim, and that Yorubas are split between Christianity and Islam.

Second, Table 4.4 indicates that a dummy variable for respondents who cited only religious differences is positive and significant. This result suggests that, all else being equal, respondents who cite only religious differences between Ghanaians

TABLE 4.3. *Probability of an Affirmative Answer to: "Do You Think Ghanaians Would Vote for a Yoruba/Hausa?" on Subsample*

	Model (1)	Model (2)	Model (3)	Model (4)	Model (5)
Yoruba	−2.013***	−2.014***	−1.980**	−1.862**	−2.018**
	(0.596)	(0.614)	(0.643)	(0.648)	(0.717)
Demographic					
Sex		−0.433	−0.295	−0.204	1.035
		(0.512)	(0.524)	(0.542)	(0.591)
Age		−0.006	−0.006	−0.025	−0.024
		(0.022)	(0.021)	(0.025)	(0.027)
Ga		−0.366	−0.502	−0.808	−0.982
		(0.599)	(0.613)	(0.720)	(0.771)
Ewe		−0.606	−0.421	−0.703	−0.822
		(0.683)	(0.673)	(0.766)	(0.746)
Enumerator bias			−1.068^	−0.908	−0.926
			(0.560)	(0.569)	(0.596)
Cosmopolitanism					
Education				−0.224	−0.196
				(0.196)	(0.187)
Years in Accra				0.020	0.022
				(0.025)	(0.025)
Nigerian area				−0.189	−0.180
				(0.524)	(0.536)
Occupation					
Unemployed					1.671
					(1.383)
Trader					0.592
					(0.621)
Constant	−0.552^	0.119	0.501	1.330	0.780
	(0.289)	(0.936)	(0.897)	(1.160)	(1.353)
Pseudo R^2	0.132	0.146	0.182	0.197	0.211
Observations	108	108	108	108	108

Robust standard errors in parentheses
Significance levels: $^\wedge p \leq 0.10$; $^* p \leq 0.05$; $^{**} p \leq 0.01$; $^{***} p \leq 0.001$.
A variable for whether the respondent was a student or not was dropped because of lack of variation on the dependent variable.

and Hausas are also more likely to claim that they would vote for a Hausa.[16] This finding supports the conjecture that interpreting Hausa as a religious identity has a positive effect on the political inclusion of Hausas. Third, even after we neutralize the "inclusionary" effect of equating Hausa with Muslim, Yorubas continue to experience greater exclusion than do Hausas in Accra society (as evidenced by the significance of the *Yoruba* coefficient).

Fourth, when we run the regression model on a subsample of Ghanaians who did not cite only religious differences between Ghanaians and Hausas, the results continue to hold (results not presented here). In other words, when we discount those respondents who are most likely to associate Hausa with merely a religious identity, we continue to find that Yorubas are more excluded by Accra society than are Hausas. These additional, stricter empirical tests suggest that the exclusion of Yorubas relative to Hausas is not merely symptomatic of the fact that Ghanaians may have confused the term *Hausa* for *Muslim*.

4.4 Conclusion

In this chapter I have addressed a number of empirical issues associated with the collection of individual-level data on voluntary migrants in a region where local understandings of ethnicity may be lost in translation. I have shown that the results in this book are not weakened or jeopardized by selection bias, geographical concerns, or questions of survey validity. By offering these additional analyses, this chapter further substantiates the claim that cultural overlap between immigrants and hosts is part of the story of immigrant exclusion and insecurity in urban West Africa.

---

[16] Note that, because respondents cited "religious differences only" for just the Hausa questionnaires, the typical method of interacting this variable with the treatment variable does not work here. Instead, the variable *Religious difference only* can already be interpreted as an interaction term: a positive value means that respondents who cited religious differences only between Hausas and Ghanaians are more accepting of Hausas than those who did not.

TABLE 4.4. *Probability of an Affirmative Answer to: "Do You Think Ghanaians Would Vote for a Yoruba/Hausa?" with Religious Difference Only Control*

	Model (1)	Model (2)	Model (3)	Model (4)	Model (5)
Yoruba	−1.384***	−1.387***	−1.429***	−1.384**	−1.409**
	(0.422)	(0.422)	(0.445)	(0.458)	(0.474)
Demographic					
Sex		0.180	0.209	0.276	0.354
		(0.385)	(0.383)	(0.400)	(0.474)
Age		0.020	0.018	0.018	0.017
		(0.016)	(0.015)	(0.020)	(0.020)
Ga		0.254	0.176	0.222	0.226
		(0.489)	(0.478)	(0.550)	(0.550)
Ewe		−0.070	−0.029	−0.036	−0.036
		(0.502)	(0.504)	(0.541)	(0.535)
Enumerator bias			−0.799^	−0.683	−0.684
			(0.422)	(0.457)	(0.455)
Cosmopolitanism					
Education				−0.107	−0.090
				(0.148)	(0.152)
Years in Accra				−0.002	−0.002
				(0.017)	(0.017)
Nigerian area				−0.196	−0.205
				(0.419)	(0.421)
Occupation					
Unemployed					0.417
					(0.881)
Trader					0.232
					(0.490)
Student					dropped
Religious difference only	2.494*	2.679*	2.261*	2.311*	2.226^
	(1.123)	(1.100)	(1.129)	(1.140)	(1.140)
Constant	−0.885***	−1.810**	−1.315^	−0.989	−1.154
	(0.234)	(0.693)	(0.733)	(0.879)	(1.028)
Pseudo R^2	0.119	0.134	0.154	0.158	0.158
Observations	191	191	191	191	189

Robust standard errors in parentheses
Significance levels: ^$p \leq$ 0.10; *$p \leq$ 0.05; **$p \leq$ 0.01; ***$p \leq$ 0.001.

The arguments advanced in Chapters 1 through 4 have a number of implications beyond the contributions they make to the immigrant question in Africa. First, they highlight the salience of ethnic and religious cleavages and institutions for social integration. Religious affiliations crosscut ethnic categories. Therefore, religious institutions could play an important role in building trust and cooperation between members of different ethnic groups. These opportunities are missed, however, when religious leaders use ethnicity as a rallying point for organization and recruitment, and effectively "ethnicize" religious institutions. The tension between the opportunities religious identities and institutions create for cooperation and their vulnerability to ethnicization is an important phenomenon in Africa today as the influences of Christianity and Islam grow.

Second, the findings in these chapters bring to light the persistent relative fragility of national identities relative to ethnic ones in West Africa. Many conversations in Accra and Niamey revealed a tendency for hosts and immigrants alike to equate national identity with ethnic identity: a Yoruba is a Nigerian, whether she is born in Ghana or in Nigeria. This is salient when the citizenship question becomes a tool to exclude candidates politically (as was attempted in Niger against President Tandja, whose father was Mauritanian) or entire ethnic groups socioeconomically (as it played out for the Burkinabés in Côte d'Ivoire).

Third, Chapters 2 through 4 provide empirical evidence that cultural differences may be endogenous to actors' strategies for highlighting cultural boundaries, consistent with Barth's initial insight that cultural identities are not objective realities but rather continuous processes of inclusion and exclusion (Barth 1969). As such, the argument presented here follows the instrumentalist school of thought on identity, which explains the construction of identity and the political salience of some cleavages over others as functions of the interests of entrepreneurs, and of the institutions they build. The research presented here further indicates that such processes carry important consequences for immigrant integration and sociopolitical stability in urban West Africa.

This book so far argues and shows that cultural overlap between immigrants and hosts has implications for immigrant exclusion. Its empirical strategy draws primarily from attitudinal indicators of immigrant attachment and host exclusion. But on a larger scale, what can we say about the determinants of anti-immigrant violence in Africa?

5

Mass Immigrant Expulsions in Africa

Samuel was born in the late 1950s in Kumasi, the capital of the Ashanti Region in what was then called the Gold Coast and what is today known as Ghana. His parents traveled from Ogbomosho in Nigeria to Ghana in the early 1930s to sell traditional Yoruba cloth. Samuel was schooled in a public school in Kumasi, where he learned the indigenous Ghanaian Ashanti language, Twi. When Samuel speaks Twi, no one can tell and no one even believes that he is of Nigerian background. In Kumasi, he and his parents attended the First Baptist Church, just like they did back in Ogbomosho, to pray with fellow Yorubas in the Yoruba language.

In November 1969, Ghana's Prime Minister Kofi Busia issued an Alien Compliance Order, giving Ghana's aliens two weeks to acquire a residence permit or leave the country. Immediately, Samuel left with his parents and siblings. They did not even try to obtain their residence permit because "during that time, most people were fearing for their lives . . . at the time, people would say 'you are aliens, go to your country!'"[1]

Between 1956 and 1999, more than 50 percent of all sub-Saharan African countries have gone through at least one mass

[1] Interview by the author, Accra, Ghana: February 5(A), 2007. "Samuel" is a pseudonym used to protect the anonymity of the respondent.

immigrant expulsion, affecting a total of approximately 3.8 million people. South Africa, Nigeria, Côte d'Ivoire, Kenya, Sierra Leone, and Uganda provide examples of countries that issued at least two mass expulsions between their independence and 1999. By contrast, Rwanda, Togo, Zimbabwe, Malawi, and Mali never resorted to such violence. The Democratic Republic of the Congo, with five expulsions, is the worst offender.

The outcomes of such expulsion events in Africa are not trivial. The average expulsion affects approximately 130,000 people, and inflicts on its victims devastating consequences, including the loss of jobs, homes, businesses, social relationships, and even personal safety. Yet scholars have argued that expulsions are costly for the expelling country as well: because many aliens in Africa are traders and entrepreneurs, expulsions disrupt economic activity. Furthermore, they may trigger a breakdown in law and order, as people take it upon themselves to implement the expulsion decree on the ground, and as demand for forged documents and for police discretion increases.[2] The evidence thus suggests that expulsions are costly for both those expelled and those doing the expelling. Why, then, do some African leaders expel their immigrants while others do not?

This chapter takes a step back from the micro-level analysis in the previous chapters to explore possible explanations of anti-immigrant violence through one indicator, mass immigrant expulsions. It highlights patterns of mass immigrant expulsions and evaluates alternative hypotheses through statistical analysis of an original dataset of mass immigrant expulsions in Africa from 1956 to 1999. It finds evidence that African leaders, particularly those from smaller ethnic groups, revert to mass immigrant expulsions in a time of economic crisis, suggesting that immigrant scapegoating in sub-Saharan Africa is alive and well.

First, I provide a descriptive summary of mass expulsions in Africa between 1956 and 1999, and explore the structural

---

[2] Peil (1971) and Himbara and Sultan (1995) discuss the consequences of expulsions.

characteristics that correlate with mass expulsions. Next, I survey
the literature for existing explanations of mass immigrant expulsions, and organize them into four families: economic, nation-
building, sociodemographic, and foreign policy. Third, I test
these competing explanations using regression analysis on the
likelihood of expulsion in any given country-year. Finally, I offer
a number of robustness checks.

5.1 Correlates of Mass Immigrant Expulsions in Africa

Mass immigrant expulsions capture one form of anti-immigrant
violence, and they are used in this chapter as an indicator of such
violence. This offers an advantage as well as a limitation. The
benefit is that a mass immigrant expulsion is an observable and
measurable event. Its use thus allows for the first systematic analysis of anti-immigrant violence in a region marred by a dearth of
reliable data. The limitation is the flip side of this: because the
data collection limits itself to an observable, measurable indicator, it naturally precludes other forms of anti-immigrant violence
that may just as well yield immigrant flows, such as purges and
pogroms.

Yet, mass expulsions offer a useful indication of immigrant
scapegoating. Indeed, Henckaerts characterizes mass expulsions
in two ways. First, a mass expulsion is an expulsion of a group
of people on the very ground of belonging to that specific group.
Second, no individual review of each expulsion is performed
(Henckaerts 1995: 21). Together, these characteristics indicate
that a mass immigrant expulsion discriminates *arbitrarily* against
specific groups of immigrants: it is thus a useful indicator of
immigrant scapegoating.

To analyze the conditions that characterize mass expulsions in a systematic manner, this chapter relies on an original
dataset of mass expulsions in all sub-Saharan African countries
between independence and 1999. The criterion for inclusion of
an expulsion episode is a mass expulsion that expelled at least

100 people.[3] Academic scholarship and media sources were used to collect the data.[4] Given that the first international treaty prohibiting mass expulsions was adopted as early as 1963, the issue of mass immigrant expulsions was likely to be on the international media's radar screen during the period covered.[5] By counting only those expulsions that affect a minimum of 100 people, the analysis distinguishes between mass expulsions – a clear form of arbitrary violence enacted at the highest level of government – and deportations, which occur on a more individual basis and are not necessarily decreed by the executive leader.

Scholars of immigration in the developing world have established that expulsions in Africa are common (Addo 1982; Ricca 1989; Weiner 1993). The dataset here identifies forty-four mass expulsions that meet the criteria listed above for the period 1956 to 1999. Most expulsions (34.09%) occurred in West Africa, but a sizable number also took place in Middle Africa (29.55%) and in East Africa (27.27%).[6] Figure 5.1 illustrates this regional variation. A plurality occurred in the 1970s (38.64%), followed by the 1980s (29.55%), the 1960s (22.73%), and finally the 1990s (9.09%). Figure 5.2 illustrates this temporal variation. The data indicate that expulsion events do not congregate in any single region of Africa or during any single decade.

Table 5.1 compares characteristics of sub-Saharan African countries that have expelled their immigrants en masse at least once between 1956 and 1999 with those of countries that have

---

[3] Sixty-one percent of all expulsions in the dataset have data on approximately how many immigrants were expelled. The remaining 39% are included because they are clearly depicted as mass expulsions, even though information on the specific number of people expelled is missing.

[4] The data on expulsions is drawn from Addo (1982); Adepoju (1984); Afolayan (1988); Gwatkin (1972); Haakonsen (1991); Henckaerts (1995); Lefebvre (2003); Rankin (2005); and Sise (1975). It also draws on news sources from Inter-Press Service, BBC, UNESCO, Agence France Press, UN Security Council, All Africa, and Radio France Internationale (data collected via Lexus-Nexus).

[5] Article 4 of the 1963 Council of Europe's second protocol proclaimed that "collective expulsion of aliens is prohibited" (Henckaerts 1995: 10).

[6] The UN Classification scheme for Africa's regional categories is used. See United Nations (2010).

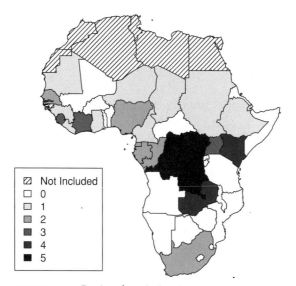

FIGURE 5.1. Regional variation in mass immigrant expulsions across sub-Saharan Africa, 1956–1999

never expelled their immigrants.[7] Countries that have expelled at least once tend to have different demographic, geographical, and ethnic characteristics from those that never expelled. Indeed, expelling countries have an average population of approximately 13 million whereas non-expelling countries have an average population of just 5 million.[8] Expelling countries tend to be closer to the equator than are non-expelling countries. Finally, compared to non-expelling countries, expelling countries have a higher index of ethnolinguistic fractionalization (0.76 versus 0.54) and a smaller plurality group size (average plurality group size of 33% versus 52%).[9] But both sets of countries are similar in their institutional framework and their experience with violence; they

---

[7] A description of each variable from Table 5.1 can be found in Appendix C.

[8] This pattern, however, may be driven by a few populous cases such as the DRC, Nigeria, Kenya, South Africa, Uganda, and Côte d'Ivoire.

[9] The ethnolinguistic fractionalization is calculated via a Herfindahl concentration index. It indicates the probability that two people in any given country, selected at random, are from different ethnic groups. It is defined as: ELF = $1 - \sum_{i=1}^{n} s_i^2$, where s_i is the share of group i ($i = 1, \ldots, n$) (see Posner 2004a).

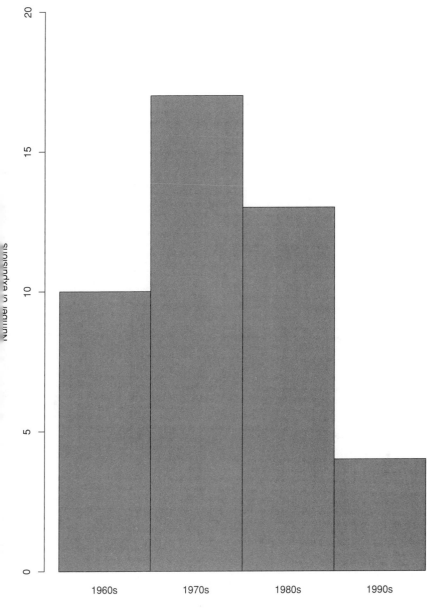

FIGURE 5.2. Number of expulsions in sub-Saharan Africa, by decade

TABLE 5.1. *Comparing Expelling Countries and Non-Expelling Countries*

	Expelling	Non-Expelling	Difference	Two-Tailed Test p-Value
Average population (millions)	13,261	5,446	7,815	0.073
Typical pop. density (*persons/km²*)	271	163	108	0.341
Area (*km²*)	710,825	424,895	285,930	0.137
Immigrant population proportion	0.038	0.049	−0.011	0.416
Absolute distance from equator	**8.36**	**13.89**	**−5.53**	**0.017**
Land boundary (*km*)	4,167	2,885	1,282	0.072
% Arable land	8.98	14.30	−5.32	0.165
% Mountainous	8.09	17.37	−9.28	0.212
Jus sanguini	0.70	0.63	0.07	0.661
French colony	0.47	0.26	0.21	0.188
British colony	0.37	0.42	−0.05	0.748
Number of war years	8.16	6.11	2.05	0.556
Number of colonial war years	5.74	4.26	1.48	0.552
ELF	**0.76**	**0.54**	**0.22**	**0.002**
Plurality group size (%)	**33**	**52**	**−19**	**0.004**
Religious fractionalization	0.51	0.47	0.04	0.523
Muslim population (%)	41.95	25.68	16.27	0.143

Statistically significant differences, at least at the 90% confidence level, are marked in **bold**.

are also not religiously dissimilar. Possible determinants of expulsion might therefore lie in a country's ability to manage its population (large populations, ethnically diverse) and in the economic conditions it faces owing to its geography.

Perhaps one of the starkest patterns that emerges from Table 5.1 is the correlation between a country's propensity to expel and its ethnic demography: on average, expelling countries have a significantly higher ethnic fractionalization index and a significantly smaller plurality group. Figure 5.3 illustrates this positive

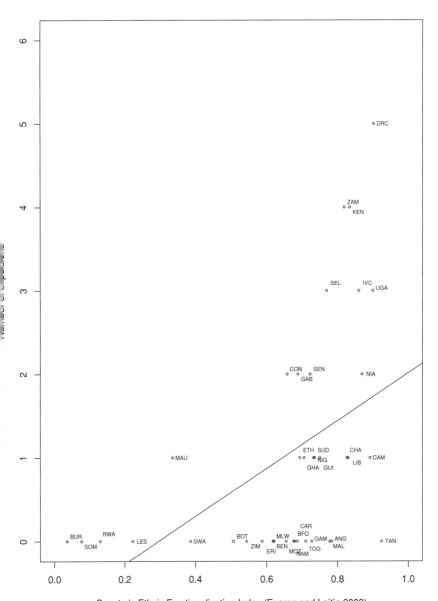

FIGURE 5.3. Correlation between a country's ethnolinguistic fractionalization and its propensity to expel

correlation between a country's index of ethnolinguistic fractionalization and the number of times it has expelled between 1956
and 1999; the Democratic Republic of the Congo, which has
expelled its immigrants en masse five times between its independence and 1999, also has one of the highest indices of ethnic
fractionalization in the region (.90): two individuals selected at
random are ethnic others 90% of the time. By contrast,
Botswana – with one of the lowest ethnic fractionalization indices
in the region (0.51) – issued no immigrant mass expulsion
between its independence and 1999. In other words, the more
ethnically diverse the country, the more mass immigrant expulsions it has enacted between 1956 and 1999.

5.2 Explaining Mass Immigrant Expulsions in Africa

The patterns presented in the previous section give us a sense
of which factors correlate with expulsion. In an effort to explain
why certain countries expel their immigrants en masse while others do not, this section turns to regression analysis to isolate
significant characteristics of expelling countries. Explanations of
mass immigrant expulsions in Africa fall into four categories:
economic, nation-building, socio-demographic, and foreign policy explanations.

Economic Explanations of Mass Expulsions

Economic arguments see the demand for, and exclusion of, immigrants as a function of an economy's needs. They are twofold:
first, that governments are more likely to enforce immigration
policy during economic downturns (Brennan 1984); and second,
that leaders are likely to blame aliens for their country's economic
ills, and therefore expel more immigrants when the economy
declines (Addo 1982; Adepoju 1984; Afolayan 1988; Brennan
1984; Peil 1971; Weiner 1993). For example, economic reasons
were cited in the expulsion of aliens, as well as nonindigenous
minorities from Ghana in 1969, Nigeria in 1983 and 1985, and
Sierra Leone in 1982. Idi Amin explicitly declared an economic

war on Uganda's Asians when he expelled close to 90,000 of them from Uganda in 1972. Figure 5.4 illustrates trends in average economic growth before and after an immigrant expulsion. Although it cannot identify causality, it highlights a clear pattern: countries tend to expel after several years of steep economic decline.[10] Whether or not economic crises actually trigger expulsions, however, is a proposition that remains to be tested empirically in a more systematic manner.

H1: The likelihood of an immigrant mass expulsion increases in times of economic crisis.

Nation-Building Explanations of Mass Expulsions

A second explanation categorizes mass immigrant expulsions as elements of a government's nation-building strategy. Governments that expel attempt to create allegiance to the nation-state (Adepoju 1984; Peil 1971), eliminate political dissidents (Weiner 1993), or purge themselves of colonial intermediaries (Challenor 1979; Ricca 1989; Weiner 1993). Adepoju's (1984) qualitative analysis of mass immigrant expulsions in Africa asserts that mass expulsions are inherently tied to the emergence of independent nation-states eager to attend to the needs of their citizens. Weiner describes the 1971 expulsion of Bengali Hindus from Pakistan as the government's attempt to quell the insurgency in the eastern part of the country (Weiner 1993). The early 1960s were marked by expulsions of Beninois nationals from Côte d'Ivoire and Niger, as these countries attempted to purge themselves of the foreigners the French colonial powers had used to staff bureaucracies (Adepoju 1984; Challenor 1979; Henckaerts 1995; Ricca 1989). An implication of this argument is that expulsions are likely to occur closer to independence and to decline in frequency with

---

[10] Figure 5.4 draws from data on GDP growth from the World Bank's World Development Indicators, accessed on October 25, 2011. These data are averaged out for the 5, 4, 3, 2, 1 year(s) preceding and succeeding an expulsion year, as well as for the expulsion year *t*, across all expelling-country cases.

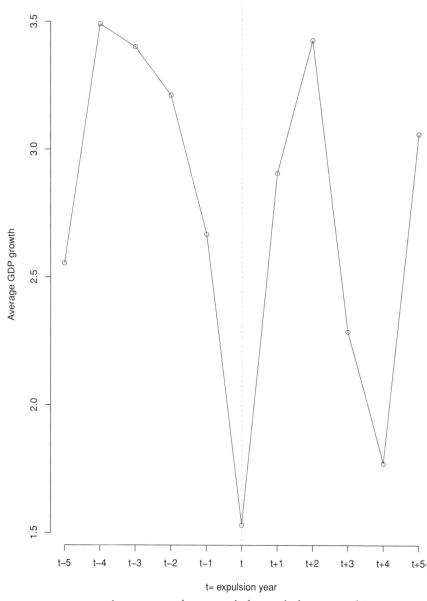

FIGURE 5.4. Average growth patterns before and after an expulsion

time. Another implication of this line of argument is that more insecure leaders are more likely to resort to immigrant mass expulsions in an effort to rally their polity around the national flag. This argument yields the following observable implications:

H2A: The likelihood of a mass expulsion decreases with time since independence.
H2B: The likelihood of a mass expulsion increases in times of political instability.

In Africa, subnational divisions tend to express themselves along cultural lines. Scholars have pointed out that these cultural, or ethnic, divisions may manifest themselves in a variety of ways, from linguistic to regional, religious, and tribal (Chazan 1982; Posner 2007). Some may be more politically salient than others (Posner 2004b). Still, this line of argument would assert that the degree of subnational fractionalization poses a challenge to national leaders. The appeal of scapegoating a common external enemy may become particularly salient for leaders facing a fractionalized ethnic landscape. Therefore, two more observable implications arise:

H2C: The likelihood of a mass expulsion increases with ethnic and cultural fractionalization, which heighten – in the leader's perception – the nation-building imperative.
H2D: Leaders facing a fractionalized ethnic landscape are more likely to revert to mass immigrant expulsions in times of vulnerability (political instability, economic slump) than are leaders facing a more homogeneous ethnic landscape.

Socio-Demographic Explanations of Mass Expulsions

A third explanation views mass immigrant expulsions as a method for population control. It explains Africa's mass immigrant expulsions as attempts to either rectify the consequences of ineffective controls at points of entry (Brennan 1984) or address social tensions such as rising crime rates by eliminating illegal aliens (Addo 1982; Adepoju 1984; Afolayan 1988; Aluko 1985). The Nigerian mass immigrant expulsion of 1983, for example, followed the Maiduguri religious riots in October 1982 in northern Nigeria. A number of non-Nigerians were allegedly implicated in these riots, exacerbating the negative image of aliens as criminal, destabilizing elements of society. This became a justification the government alluded to when it decreed the expulsion (Aluko 1985). This explanation yields the following observable implications:

H3A: The likelihood of a mass expulsion increases under demographic pressure.

H3B: The likelihood of a mass expulsion increases after an influx of immigrants.[11]

Foreign Policy Explanations of Mass Expulsions

A final explanation for why African countries expel their immigrants en masse portrays immigrant mass expulsions as elements of a country's foreign policy. According to this argument, countries expel their immigrants to put pressure on neighboring states, or to antagonize the country whose nationals are targeted in the event (Weiner 1993). For example, Aluko (1985) interprets the expulsion of Ghanaians from Nigeria in the early 1980s as reciprocation for Ghana's 1969 expulsion of Nigerians. This explanation would predict a greater likelihood of mass immigrant expulsions between countries that harbor a history of antagonistic relations, and yields the following observable implication:

H4: The likelihood of an immigrant mass expulsion is higher in a country A of nationals from country B, where country B previously expelled nationals from country A.

5.3 Testing the Arguments

The main hypotheses in this chapter (H1 through H4) focus on the competing roles that economic growth, nation-building, socio-demographic pressure, and foreign policy play in predicting

---

[11] One additional hypothesis would claim that the likelihood of a mass expulsion increases in times of increasing crime rates. However, this cannot be tested given the dearth of crime data in Africa over time.

mass expulsion. To evaluate these competing explanations, this chapter relies on a country-year analysis that estimates the likelihood of expulsion in any given year, hence capturing time-variant factors.[12] The dependent variable, *Expulsion*, is coded "1" for all country-years in which expulsions occurred, and "0" otherwise.

Operationalizing the Economic Argument

The claim that immigrant mass expulsions increase in times of economic crisis (H1) is tested using a basic measure of change in economic growth preceding the expulsion. According to Figure 5.4, per capita gross domestic product tends to decline in the years preceding an expulsion. That decline is steepest in the two years preceding an expulsion. Therefore, *Two-year growth change* captures the difference between growth in the expulsion year and growth two years prior to the expulsion year. It is constructed based on data on Africa's per capita gross domestic product from Miguel et al. (2004). If (H1) is correct, we expect to find a significant negative effect of the two-year growth change on the probability of expulsion.

Operationalizing the Nation-Building Argument

The hypothesis that expulsions decrease with time since independence (H2a) is tested using *Independent years*, a continuous variable that counts, for each country-year, the number of years since a country's independence. If (H2a) is correct, we should find a significant negative effect of the number of independent years on the likelihood of expulsion. The hypothesis that mass expulsions increase in times of political instability (H2b) is tested using a lagged measure of political instability at the center, *Instability* (Fearon and Laitin 2003).[13] If (H2b) is correct, we should see a significant positive effect of political instability on the likelihood

---

[12] The model here follows models used for analyzing the determinants of civil war. See, for example, Fearon and Laitin (2003).

[13] This is a dummy variable indicating whether, in any of the three preceding years, the country experienced a change of three units or more on the Polity IV regime index (Fearon and Laitin 2003: 81).

of expulsion. The claim that mass expulsions increase with ethnic fractionalization (H2c) is tested using *Leader group prop.*, the population share of the leader's ethnic group. This measure is used instead of the conventional Atlas Narodov Mira index of ethnic fractionalization, which is time-invariant. The two variables are significantly correlated with each other ($r = -0.4492$, $p < 0.000$), indicating that ethnically fractionalized countries are also more likely to produce leaders from smaller ethnic bases. If (H2c) is correct, we should see a significant negative effect of a leader's ethnic group share on the likelihood of expulsion. Finally, the conditional effect of nation-building attempts based on the ethnic landscape a leader faces is tested with three interaction terms. *LeaderGpPropXGrowth* captures the interaction between a leader's ethnic group proportion and the two-year economic growth change. *LeaderGpPropXInstab* captures the interaction between a leader's ethnic group proportion and political instability at the center. *LeaderGpPropXIndep* captures the interaction between a leader's ethnic group proportion and the number of years since the country's independence.

Operationalizing the Socio-Demographic Argument

The claim that mass expulsions increase under demographic pressure (H3a) is tested using the lag of the rate of change in population, *Pop. rate chg.*, and controlling for that country's initial population level: the second lag of its population, *Pop.* (Fearon and Laitin 2003). If (H3a) is correct, we should see a significant positive effect of the rate of change in population on the likelihood of expulsion.

Alternatively, mass expulsions may be used as a tool to manage migration flows. In other words, leaders may rely on mass expulsions to rectify inadequate borders at points of entry. Although data on migration flows over time in sub-Saharan Africa are lacking, it remains possible to test this argument by evaluating the effects of migrant pull-factors. Two sources of migrant-labor lie in the agricultural and mining sectors: if mass expulsions are used as a tool to manage migration flows, we expect their likelihood to increase after the pull of an oil and/or agricultural boom. Thus, (H3b) is tested using two indicators. *Oil* captures the lag in the deviation in oil exports relative to the country's average oil exports for the entire period (Fearon and Laitin 2003). *Precip.* captures the lag in the deviation in precipitation relative to the country's average precipitation for the entire period.[14] If (H3b) is correct, we should find significant positive effects of *Oil* and *Precipitation* on the likelihood of expulsion.

Finally, H4 cannot be tested statistically with this dataset.[15] A qualitative discussion of the claim that expulsions are part of a nation's foreign policy (H4) follows the statistical analysis.

Statistical Results

In Table 5.2, each column tests hypotheses (H1) through (H3b) individually, and the last column tests all hypotheses jointly. Furthermore, each model includes country fixed effects and country-year time trends. The former accounts for time-invariant country-specific factors that might explain baseline differences in countries' propensity to expel immigrants. The latter accounts for country-specific time-variant factors.[16] Finally, each model is run using a specification that clusters the standard errors at the country-level and a specification that does not; clustering at the country-level accounts for the fact that different observations for the same country may not be independent from one another. However, clustering does not allow for the computation of a Wald-chi-square test statistic, which speaks to the overall statistical significance of the model. Therefore, both specifications are run, but only the results from the non-clustering specification

---

[14] Precipitation and oil are specified as their deviation from their average over the entire time period, in order to capture – not long-run trends – but rather year-to-year deviations from what is expected. Robustness checks, later in the chapter, consider different specifications for these indicators.

[15] There is not enough information on the national origins of those targeted in an expulsion to adequately test this hypothesis in the regression.

[16] This follows other work on the causes of civil conflict in Africa (Burke et al. 2009; Miguel et al. 2004).

are reported and only statistically significant coefficients in both specifications are considered.

Table 5.2 gives us a sense of how well each explanation fares both individually, and jointly in the full model. It indicates that each family of explanations carries some weight in a statistical regression. As we first noticed in Figure 5.4, a decrease in economic growth in the two years preceding an expulsion significantly increases the probability of expulsion. This result is statistically significant at the 90 percent confidence level when tested individually, and at the 99 percent confidence level when tested jointly against all other explanations.[17] Furthermore, a likelihood-ratio test comparing the full model (H3) to one that excludes the economic predictor indicates that including the economic variable results in a statistically significant improvement in model fit, at the 99 percent confidence level.

Are expulsions characteristic of a young or weakened government's nation-building strategy (H2a through H2d)? Instability at the center and time since independence exercise statistically insignificant effects. Furthermore, a time-variant indicator of ethnic fractionalization, the population share of the leader's ethnic group, indicates that while leaders from larger ethnic groups are less likely to expel their immigrants, this effect is not statistically significant. These results provide no significant support for the claim that mass expulsions are part of a larger nation-building strategy.[18]

However, column (H2d) reveals a conditional effect of nation-building strategies on mass immigrant expulsions. The significant, positive interaction between a leader's ethnic group share and the two-year growth change indicates that the economic trigger for a mass expulsion goes into effect only for leaders from small ethnic groups, not for leaders from large ethnic groups. Table 5.3 illustrates this conditional effect more clearly

---

[17] The specification that clusters the standard errors by country yields the same results, with an increased confidence level on *Two-year growth change* to 95% in Model (H1).

[18] The specification that clusters the standard errors by country yields the same results.

TABLE 5.2. *Probability of Expansion in Any Given Country-Year*

	Economic	Nation-Building				Socio-Demographic		Full
	(H1)	(H2a)	(H2b)	(H2c)	(H2d)	(H3a)	(H3b)	(H1-3)
Two-year growth change	-2.954^				-7.178**			-7.531**
	(1.590)				(2.465)			(2.587)
Independent years		-0.018			-0.213*			-0.079
		(0.041)			(0.098)			(0.131)
Instability (lagged)			-0.430		-1.515^			-1.209
			(0.492)		(0.849)			(0.917)
Leader group prop.				-2.430	-11.659			-7.890
				(3.811)	(7.801)			(8.287)
LeaderGpPropXGrowth					30.400**			32.282**
					(11.243)			(11.581)
LeaderGpPropXInstab					4.879			3.110
					(3.908)			(4.264)
LeaderGpPropXIndep					0.575^			0.470
					(0.299)			(0.314)
Pop. (lagged twice)						-0.001		-0.001
						(0.000)		(0.001)
Pop. rate chg. (lagged)						8.042		24.784
						(12.974)		(24.430)
Precip. (lagged dev.)							0.003*	0.004*
							(0.001)	(0.002)
Oil (lagged dev.)							2.585**	1.602
							(0.966)	(1.435)
Pseudo R^2	0.175	0.120	0.132	0.121	0.217	0.164	0.156	0.259
Wald Chi^2	538.91	172.53	164.64	169.36	699.38	137.89	174.41	657.40
Observations	774	852	829	849	769	810	831	769

Robust standard errors in parentheses. All models include country fixed effects and country-year time trends.

Significance levels: ^ $p \leq 0.10$; * $p \leq 0.05$; ** $p \leq 0.01$; *** $p \leq 0.001$.

TABLE 5.3. *Illustrating the Interaction Effect on the Probability of Expulsion (%)*

		Leader Group Proportion	
		Low	High
Two-year growth change	Negative	4.65	1.62
		[3.29; 6.54]	[0.85; 3.05]
	Positive	3.23	1.65
		[2.10; 4.94]	[0.94; 2.88]

by showing the predicted probability of expulsion under four different hypothetical scenarios (low leader ethnic share + economic decline, low leader ethnic share + economic growth, high leader ethnic share + economic decline, and high leader ethnic share + economic growth). It indicates that the greatest probability of expulsion (4.65%) occurs in countries that are experiencing economic hardship and whose leader's ethnic share is low. By contrast, the probability of expulsion drops by more than one percentage point, to 3.23 percent, when the leader's ethnic share is low but the country is experiencing economic growth. Finally, when a leader's ethnic share is high, economic patterns seem to matter less and the likelihood of expulsion drops to just over 1.6 percent.[19] Leaders with a small ethnic base are thus more prone to expel their immigrants en masse, particularly when they face poor economic conditions. Leaders with a large ethnic base, on the other hand, tend to expel their immigrants en masse a lot

---

[19] The probabilities and 95% confidence intervals in Table 5.3 are calculated via *Stata*'s post-estimation tools on a simple logistic model of *Expulsion* on *Two-year growth change*, *Leader group prop.* and the interaction of the two: *LeaderGpPropXGrowth*. The 95% confidence bounds on the prediction are then transformed back through an inverse log. High leader group proportion is 40%, the 75th percentile for the sample; low leader group proportion is 8.5%, the 25th percentile for the sample. High growth change is 0.05 percentage points, the 75th percentile for the sample; low growth change is −0.05 percentage points, the 25th percentile for the sample.

less often, and seem not to condition that decision on the recent economic health of their country. In their decision to expel immigrants, leaders facing a more fractionalized ethnic landscape are more sensitive to changes in their economy than are leaders facing a more homogeneous ethnic landscape.[20] A likelihood-ratio test comparing the full model to one that excludes the nation-building variables indicates, with 90% confidence, that adding the nation-building variables results in a statistically significant improvement in model fit.

Does socio-demographic pressure increase the likelihood of expulsion? Column (H3a) in Table 5.2 finds no support for a significant effect of the rate of change in the population on the likelihood of expulsion. Although the coefficient has the expected, positive sign, it is not statistically distinguishable from zero. However, column (H3b) indicates that demographic pressure from in-migration does hold a statistically significant effect on the likelihood of mass expulsion. Mass immigrant expulsions are more likely after a strong agricultural or mining year. The effect of precipitation, in particular, is robust in the full model.[21] Furthermore, a likelihood-ratio test comparing the full model to one that excludes the socio-demographic variables indicates, at the 99 percent confidence level, that adding the socio-demographic variables results in a statistically significant improvement in model fit.

Model (H1-3) tests (H1) through (H3) simultaneously. Results indicate that the patterns most robust to the full set of controls are the direct effect of economic growth, the conditional effect of growth based on the leader's ethnic group share, and the positive effect of precipitation. The p-value for the Wald-statistic indicates that this full model is statistically significant ($p < 0.0000$), and the Pseudo R^2 indicates that it explains just over

---

[20] The specification that clusters the standard errors by country yields the same results.

[21] The specification that clusters the standard errors by country yields the same results.

one-quarter of the variation in mass expulsions across sub-Saharan Africa between 1956 and 1999. The typical expelling country is a country whose ethnic minority leader, following the pull of an agricultural-boom year, faces difficult economic conditions.[22]

Finally, are expulsions used as a foreign policy tool to target nationals of an antagonistic country? In other words, do leaders play tit-for-tat with one another, using immigrants as their foreign policy tool? Some scholars claim, for example, that the expulsion of Ghanaians from Nigeria in the early 1980s was reciprocation for Ghana's 1969 expulsion of Nigerians (Aluko 1985). Such an explanation would predict a greater likelihood of mass immigrant expulsions between countries that harbor a history of antagonistic immigrant relations. This hypothesis cannot be tested statistically, but it is addressed qualitatively here. Of the 40 expulsion events that allegedly targeted specific groups, only two were part of tit-for-tat strategies: the Nigerian expulsion of Ghanaians in the 1980s; and the 1989 expulsion of 90,000 Mauritanians from Senegal, which took place just a few days after the Senegalese government expelled approximately 70,000 Mauritanians because of a grazing rights dispute over the Senegal river (Henckaerts 1995). Beyond these two episodes, only two other instances of mass expulsions appear to be symptomatic of antagonistic relations between two countries: the 1964 expulsion of Congolese and Burundian immigrants from the DRC and the 1978 expulsion of Beninois immigrants from Gabon. The DRC claimed that its Congolese and Burundian immigrants were supporting rebel forces against the government (Sise 1975). Gabon's expulsion was symptomatic of the hostile relations that Gabon and Benin fostered over fishing disputes (Henckaerts 1995; Haakonsen 1991). These examples corroborate the claim that mass immigrant expulsions are part of a country's foreign policy strategy toward nationals of antagonistic countries, but they constitute only 10 percent of all targeted expulsions.

---

[22] The specification that clusters the standard errors by country yields similar results.

5.4 Robustness Checks

The statistical analysis so far indicates that expulsions follow (1) an economic crisis, particularly in countries where leaders stem from a small ethnic base, and (2) an increase in precipitation. This section tests the stability of these patterns by offering a number of robustness tests. Specifically, the following checks are run. First, alternative constructs are used for growth, as well as precipitation and oil. For example, does the effect of GDP growth change if we look at four-year growth rates, or at the lag of GDP growth? Second, the model is run using a dummy variable, rather than a continuous measure, for the leader's ethnic group share. Third, additional controls are placed on the right-hand side. Fourth, the model is stripped to its bare essentials: growth, the leader's ethnic group share, and the interaction of the two. Finally, a linear specification of the model is run in order to avoid inconsistent estimators, which arise for logit specifications with fixed effects.[23] All models include country fixed effects and country-year time trends. All models are run with and without clustered standard errors at the country level, and only results that apply to both specifications are reported.

In a first robustness test, alternative constructs for growth, precipitation and oil are used. For GDP per capita, the change in growth in the four years preceding the expulsion (rather than in the two years preceding the expulsion), the lagged growth and the lagged deviation in growth are used. None yield a statistically significant effect. Only the two-year change yields a

---

[23] Ideally, an additional robustness check instrumenting for the two-year change in per capita GDP would be run, to account for potential simultanity in the relationship between GDP and expulsion. Rainfall has previously been used to instrument for per capita GDP in Africa (Miguel et al. 2004). However, rainfall is correlated with expulsions and thus cannot be used as an instrument here. Alternatively, temperature – as a variable that is not correlated with expulsions but that is correlated with growth – could be used as an instrument. Various model specifications were run, but the F-statistic on the first-stage is consistently small, never surpassing 3. This indicates that temperature is a weak instrument for estimating the effect of exogenous changes in per capita GDP growth on expulsion.

consistently significant effect on the likelihood of expulsion. By contrast, when lagged measures of oil and precipitation levels are used (rather than lagged deviations from the average), the patterns previously uncovered persist: oil and precipitation have a positive and statistically significant effect. In sum, the effect of GDP per capita growth is specific to the two-year change specification, a pattern we originally observed in Figure 5.4; but the effect of precipitation and oil is robust to different variable constructs.

Second, a set of robustness checks relying on a dichotomous rather than a continuous measure of the leader's ethnic group proportion yields results that are similar to those in (H1) through (H1-3). An *Ethnic Dummy* variable is defined as "0" if the leader's ethnic group share is less than 0.27, the mean for the entire sample; and "1" if the leader's ethnic group share is equal to, or greater than, 0.27. Results indicate that GDP per capita growth holds a negative and statistically significant effect, precipitation and oil have a positive and statistically significant effect, and the interaction between the leader's ethnic group share and per capita GDP growth holds a positive and statistically significant effect.[24] In short, the main results persist.

Third, the model is run with additional controls for a country's political institutions and previous experience with violence. Political institutions are operationalized in a number of different ways. First, a simple aggregate *Polity score*, which summarizes the extent to which the regime comprises autocratic versus democratic features, is included. Second, the analysis controls instead for dichotomous measures of democracy and anocracy – with autocracy as the omitted category. Third, rather than relying on rough measures of regime-type, the analysis controls for a more fine-grained measure of political institutions provided by the

---

[24] Note that in these tests, the interaction between the leader's ethnic group share and the number of years since independence is also positive and statistically significant. However, this result is not robust in other tests, nor is it significant in the full model (H1-3) in Table 5.2.

World Bank: whether the system is parliamentary or presidential.[25] Finally, the analysis controls for two leader characteristics that might be associated with a greater tendency to rely on mass expulsions: whether the executive is a military officer, and the number of years the leader has been in office.[26] None of these variables reach statistical significance. Furthermore, the main results hold in the full 1956–1999 sample.[27] Finally, a country's previous experience with violence is captured by two dichotomous measures: whether, in the previous year, the country experienced war and whether it experienced an expulsion. These factors do not hold statistically significant effects on the likelihood of expulsion. Furthermore, all the patterns in (H1-3) hold. Results from these robustness checks are presented in Table 5.4.

Fourth, the model is stripped to its bare essentials to test whether the main results – the conditional effect of growth by the leader's ethnic population share – are stable in the simplest of specifications. The effect remains statistically significant at least at the 99 percent confidence level.

Finally, the model is run as an ordinary least squares specification rather than a logit. A logit with fixed effects may be inconsistent. To avoid this, I run the OLS specification on both the bare essentials model (including only the two-year growth change, the leader's ethnic share, the interaction of the two, and

---

[25] The World Bank Political Institutions Database (Beck et al. 2001) describes regimes as parliamentary, presidential, or assembly-elected presidential. Three dichotomous variables are created to capture each type: in the regression, the omitted category is *Presidential*.

[26] *Polity score*, *Democracy* and *Anocracy* are from Fearon and Laitin (2003). *Parliamentary*, *Presidential*, *Military executive*, and *Leader tenure* are from Beck et al. (2001). Note that the World Bank Political Institutions Database collects data only from 1975 onward.

[27] One reason why political institutions have no significant effect may be that the model controls for country specific time-variant factors. Note that in Models (3) and (4), the sample is truncated to 1975–1999. It is therefore unsurprising that the main effects lose their statistical significance. Furthermore, the effect of oil flips direction; this may be due to the changing dynamics of petro-politics since the 1970s oil booms.

TABLE 5.4. *Probability of Expulsion in Any Given Country-Year –
Robustness Checks*

	Indep. – 1999 (1)	Indep. – 1999 (2)	1975 – 1999 (3)	1975 – 1999 (4)	Indep. – 1999 (5)
Two-year growth change	−7.936**	−8.176**	−4.343	−4.732	−7.896**
	(2.745)	(2.697)	(3.589)	(3.283)	(2.552)
Leader group prop.	1.268	0.380	4.075	0.958	0.023
	(4.852)	(5.138)	(6.631)	(6.377)	(4.127)
LeaderGpPropXGrowth	32.751**	33.371**	16.266	17.297	33.195**
	(12.792)	(12.288)	(13.097)	(13.483)	(12.549)
Precip. (lagged dev.)	0.004*	0.004*	0.004*	0.004*	0.003*
	(0.002)	(0.002)	(0.002)	(0.002)	(0.002)
Oil (lagged dev.)	2.131^	2.298*	−11.201***	−13.357***	2.241^
	(1.189)	(1.147)	(1.679)	(1.610)	(1.192)
Polity (lagged)	−0.036				
	(0.082)				
Democracy (lagged)		0.494			
		(1.208)			
Anocracy (lagged)		−0.718			
		(0.698)			
Parliamentary (lagged)			2.187		
			(2.373)		
Assembly (lagged)			3.892		
			(2.505)		
Military executive				−1.356	
				(1.250)	
Years in office				−0.087	
				(0.059)	
Conflict (lagged)					0.641
					(0.871)
Expulsion (lagged)					−0.602
					(0.653)
Pseudo R^2	0.221	0.227	0.241	0.225	0.225
Wald Chi^2	695.35	624.06	224.99	266.33	660.72
Observations	769	769	363	377	771

Robust standard errors in parentheses. All models include country fixed effects and country-year
time trends. Significance levels: ^$p \leq 0.10$; *$p \leq 0.05$; **$p \leq 0.01$; ***$p \leq 0.001$.

country fixed effects as well as country-year time trends) and the
full model (H1-3) from Table 5.2. The results remain robust: in
specifications that cluster the standard errors at the country level
and specifications that do not cluster the standard errors at the

country-level, the two-year change in growth has a negative and statistically significant effect (at least at the 90 percent confidence level); and the interaction between growth and the leader's ethnic group share has a positive and statistically significant effect (at least at the 95 percent confidence level). Finally, precipitation has a positive and statistically significant (at least at the 95 percent confidence level) effect on expulsion.

The robustness checks in this section have tested to see whether the patterns uncovered in (H1) through (H1-3) are robust to the most parsimonious specification, to a fuller specification, to alternative variable constructs, and to a linear specification. The results indicate that these patterns are robust, and increase our confidence that leaders emanating from a small ethnic base and facing a severe drop in GDP per capita over two years are more likely to revert to mass immigrant expulsions. Table 5.5 summarizes these results.

5.5 Conclusion

Mass immigrant expulsions have significant implications for immigrants and host countries alike. Countries that expel their immigrants forfeit significant economic opportunities. Expelled immigrants also lose important sources of livelihood in their rush to exit a suddenly hostile environment. Yet more than forty expulsion events occurred in sub-Saharan African countries from independence to 1999, and more than half of sub-Saharan African countries expelled their immigrants at least once. This chapter has offered an analysis of such events and highlighted a number of phenomena.

First, the analysis here demonstrates that while mass immigrant expulsions are a recurring occurrence in the region, they vary widely by country. Some countries, such as Tanzania, Namibia, and Mali, have never expelled their immigrants; others, such as Kenya, Côte d'Ivoire, and the Democratic Republic of the Congo, have done so regularly. Second, the analysis in this chapter highlights a number of significant trends related to mass immigrant expulsions: expelling countries tend to be

TABLE 5.5. *Summary of Regression Results*

Explanation	Hypothesis	Expected Effect	Result
Economic	(H1): The likelihood of an immigrant mass expulsion increases in times of economic crisis	Negative	✓
Nation-building	(H2a): The likelihood of an immigrant mass expulsion decreases with time since independence	Negative	–
	(H2b): The likelihood of an immigrant mass expulsion increases in times of political instability	Positive	–
	(H2c): The likelihood of an immigrant mass expulsion increases with ethnic fractionalization	Positive	–
	(H2d): Leaders facing a fractionalized ethnic landscape are more likely to revert to mass immigrant expulsions in times of vulnerability	Positive	✓
Socio-demographic	(H3a): The likelihood of an immigrant mass expulsion increases under demographic pressure	Positive	–
	(H3b): The likelihood of an immigrant mass expulsion increases after an influx of immigrants	Positive	✓

more populous, closer to the equator, and more ethnically diverse. Third, mass expulsions are driven by economic, nation-building, and socio-demographic pressures. More specifically, mass expulsions follow a two-year decline in per capita economic growth, and leaders belonging to relatively small ethnic groups are driving this pattern. These empirical results are consistent with a story of immigrant scapegoating: ethnic minority leaders tend to revert to immigrant expulsions in times of economic decline.[28]

These results are certainly not deterministic, but they do offer a preliminary understanding of a little-studied phenomenon in Africa. Among other things, they underscore the challenges that African societies and polities face in integrating new forms of diversity. This poses a dilemma: African economies have perhaps the most to gain from immigrant economic activity, and yet are most vulnerable to the tensions that immigration creates.

The results in this chapter also qualify popular economic accounts of immigrant scapegoating. While economic competition no doubt fuels anti-immigrant sentiment, it only yields political violence against immigrants to the extent that it interacts with the ethnic landscape of a country. A leader's decision to expel his immigrants en masse is not merely a direct response to economic pressure; rather, it represents a more complex calculus that takes into account the ethnic landscape the leader faces.

---

[28] In a book comparing the development of racial policy making in Brazil, the United States, and South Africa, Marx (1998) argues that the United States and South Africa instituted racism in an effort to unite an otherwise fragmented white population, suggesting that leaders overcome internal divisions by sharpening boundaries. A similar logic would explain why leaders with a smaller ethnic base are also more likely to sharpen boundaries with immigrants, via mass expulsions.

6

Conclusion

I studied two immigrant communities in three West African cities to learn why groups that appear to be most likely to assimilate end up facing greater exclusion than groups that are more easily labeled as foreigners. I learned that the immigrant integration process in urban West Africa pits the incentives of individual immigrants trying to assimilate against those of immigrant leaders protecting their groups as well as their own positions of power. Leaders resist immigrant assimilation because they benefit both socially and materially from their leadership position over a distinct immigrant community. They counter the threat of assimilation by striking bargains with local police to become monopoly providers of social and civil protection for their immigrants, thus gaining the leverage they need to lock in immigrant loyalty and membership through formal organizations and institutions. Furthermore, hosts who compete economically with immigrant traders adopt exclusionary attitudes toward immigrant groups whose capacity to assimilate poses a socioeconomic threat. As a result, religious or ethnic similarities between immigrants and hosts are neither necessary nor sufficient for immigrant integration. In fact, cultural similarity can disrupt integration: the high-overlap immigrants studied in this book are more excluding and more excluded. In times of political instability, they are also more insecure.

Economic and cultural factors are thus deeply intertwined in explaining the immigrant integration process in urban West Africa. This holds when we aim to understand broader patterns of anti-immigrant violence in the region: a systematic analysis of new data on mass immigrant expulsions in Africa shows that leaders facing an ethnically fractionalized landscape turn to mass immigrant expulsions after a couple years of economic decline.

These findings bring perspective to the literature on the determinants of immigrant exclusion in industrialized democracies. Today, this literature is divided into two camps: the cultural threat argument and the economic threat argument. The former points to cultural factors as determinants of immigrant exclusion (Sniderman et al. 2004; Hainmueller and Hiscox 2007; Hainmueller and Hangartner 2013) while the latter highlights economic competition as its source (Dancygier 2010; Malhotra et al. 2013). This book investigates the extent to which such arguments travel to the African region. Its findings highlight the fact that, in West Africa, *both* cultural and economic factors are at play; in fact, the two are difficult to disentangle. At the micro-level, cultural networks act as economic assets in the competition for supplies, credit, and customers; and cultural overlap, an important potential asset for immigrants, represents an economic threat to indigenous traders with whom immigrants compete. At the macro-level, ethnic fractionalization interacts with economic decline to explain mass immigrant expulsions. Indeed, the effect of GDP per capita in the two years preceding a mass expulsion is significantly mediated by the size of a leader's ethnic base, such that only leaders stemming from a relatively small ethnic group scapegoat their immigrants in a time of economic crisis. Pitting the economic story against the cultural story is thus not a constructive approach for understanding immigrant exclusion in Africa. In a region where cultural networks underpin many economic transactions, cultural and economic threats are one and the same.

The findings in this book bridge two more literatures. Scholars who study immigrant integration in industrialized countries emphasize an immigrant's ability to assimilate, through host language acquisition or cultural adaptation for example, as a factor contributing to immigrant acceptance and integration (Alba and Nee 2003; Gradstein and Schiff 2006; Horowitz 1985; Huntington 1996; Sniderman et al. 2004). Yet a different literature on identity formation and intergroup relations informs us that cultural boundaries may be endogenous and that they are shaped largely by the incentives and strategies of cultural entrepreneurs (Barth 1969; Fearon and Laitin 1996; Laitin 1998). This literature conceptualizes cultural entrepreneurs as agents with an incentive to create group boundaries, either out of egotistical incentives – they stand to gain financially or socially as leaders of a distinct group – or altruistic concerns – they help facilitate intergroup cooperation. The findings in this book thus challenge the conventional wisdom in the immigrant integration literature by applying the ethnic entrepreneur approach to the study of immigrant incorporation in Africa. In a setting where state capacity is weak and government immigration policy nonexistent, this book borrows insights from the literature on identity formation to emphasize the role of local actors in determining immigrant exclusion through the creation and recreation of group boundaries. By doing so, this book extends the reach of the identity formation literature to the context of immigrant exclusion in urban West Africa.

Finally, the research in this book contributes to the rich literature on citizenship in Africa, which already informs us of the depth and diversity of human mobility, migration, and exclusion in the region (de Bruijn et al. 2001). Through a micro-level analysis of two migrant ethnic groups in three West African cities, this book goes beyond single case studies to offer a theory of immigrant exclusion in urban centers. It thus begins to highlight those factors we might want to account for when we try to understand patterns of exclusion across the region. However, barring a large-N analysis of immigrant exclusion by immigrant ethnic group, this argument is not yet generalizable to the entire region. Future research should aim to offer a direct test of economic and cultural determinants of immigrant exclusion across immigrant groups, African countries, and years.

Many more questions remain unanswered still. First, do exclusionary attitudes toward immigrants vary across indigenous ethnic or religious groups? Some of the empirical results presented, but not discussed, in this book suggest that some ethnic or occupational groups – the Ewes in Accra and the traders in Niamey – are more excluding than others. Are these results indicative of a larger trend, whereby minority ethnic groups or workers who compete directly with immigrants are more excluding? Although the results in this book suggest that some social and economic groups may be more excluding than others, they merely bring to our attention the heterogeneity of host societies. A study devoted entirely to divergent exclusionary attitudes across indigenous groups is critical for understanding group relations in localities that are socially diverse and economically underdeveloped.

Second, under what circumstances does anti-immigrant sentiment translate into anti-immigrant behavior? Chapters 2 and 3 focus on anti-immigrant sentiment. Chapter 5, and the discussion of the Alien Compliance Order in Ghana throughout the book, explore the determinants of anti-immigrant behavior, namely mass expulsions. This raises the question: When mass immigrant expulsions arise, do they target high-overlap groups? The Ghana ACO case suggests that they do. But a systematic analysis of anti-immigrant violence from the immigrant group perspective is important for our understanding of the immigrant experience in the developing world.

Third, if cultural similarity can both improve and worsen group relations, how might we identify the circumstances under which one effect dominates the other? This book defines specific scope conditions where immigrant integration is a local-level, informal phenomenon shaped by immigrant community leaders and host police rather than by government policy. The counterintuitive finding that cultural similarities exacerbate immigrant exclusion is specific to these scope conditions. An extension of this research might identify conditions elsewhere and at different points in time, which mirror those in urban West Africa today, and ask to what extent the same dynamics apply. How did German immigrants fare relative to Irish immigrants in nineteenth-century New York City? How might this book's story shed light on religious conflict and tolerance in Europe between the Reformation and the French Revolution? More generally, when do shared cultural traits exacerbate group relations and when do they improve them?

Although numerous questions remain, this book has begun to shed light on the immigrant experience in the developing world, an issue of great relevance for the economic and sociopolitical stability of African countries. As regional integration expands in sub-Saharan Africa – a trend we are already witnessing with the increasing salience of regional blocs such as ECOWAS (the Economic Community of West African States) and SADC (the Southern African Development Community) – borders will grow more porous and worker mobility more fluid. But as long as immigrants find protection and security only through the bargains their leaders strike with local authorities, they cannot settle and operate in their host economies with long-term horizons. Governments that are capable of formalizing the immigration process and offering a more stable and reliable source of security to their immigrants will better capitalize on the immigrant potential for economic growth by encouraging local and longer-term investments in host societies. As these governments play a greater role in enforcing the rule of law, the importance of local entrepreneurs such as immigrant community leaders will wane because immigrants will find security through formal-legal means rather than kinship ties. Over time, if states and national identities gain strength, the dynamics explored and explained in this book will likely transition to what we observe today in industrialized democracies. The consolidation of the nation-state in sub-Saharan Africa will therefore carry significant implications for the fate of Africa's immigrants.

Appendixes

A. Constructing the Immigrant Attachment Index

TABLE A.1. *Immigrant Attachment Index Construction: Yorubas and Hausas in Accra, Cotonou, and Niamey*

	Accra		Cotonou		Niamey	
	Yoruba	Hausa	Yoruba	Hausa	Yoruba	Hausa
Went back to Nigeria over previous month	0.11	0.04	0.32	0.27	0.04	0.23
Voted in last Nigerian presidential elections	0.16	0.06	0.57	0.33	0.11	0.30
Currently sends remittances back to Nigeria	0.53	0.16	0.87	0.73	0.91	0.57
Has tribal marks	0.05	0.28	0.26	0.07	0.40	0.47
Acquired current job through coethnic	0.42	0.54	0.48	0.80	0.48	0.33
Children school(ed) only in Nigeria	0.10	0.04	0.31	0.33	0.20	0.27
Holds Nigerian passport	0.37	0.06	0.31	0.07	0.39	0.30
Follows Nigerian news daily	0.40	0.54	0.67	0.70	0.37	0.80
Identifies as Nigerian over host country national	0.53	0.06	0.96	0.73	0.91	0.90
Average	0.30	0.20	0.53	0.45	0.42	0.46

TABLE A.2. *Immigrant Attachment Index Construction: Christian and Muslim Yorubas in Accra*

	Christian Yoruba	Muslim Yoruba
Went back to Nigeria over previous month	0.13	0.08
Voted in last Nigerian presidential elections	0.24	0.05
Currently sends remittances back to Nigeria	0.72	0.29
Has tribal marks	0.02	0.10
Acquired current job through coethnic	0.54	0.31
Children school(ed) only in Nigeria	0.13	0.07
Holds Nigerian passport	0.56	0.14
Follows Nigerian news daily	0.41	0.37
Identifies as Nigerian over host country national	0.76	0.24
Average	**0.39**	**0.18**

B. Constructing the Cultural Overlap Index

Cultural overlap is considered a dichotomous measure in this book. Some immigrants share higher levels of cultural overlap with their hosts than do others. Another way to think about this concept is as a continuous measure. Table B.1 illustrates how one might construct such a measure, and it is based on demographic proportions from the surveys of immigrant and host populations introduced in this book.

TABLE B.1. *Overlap Index Construction*

	Accra		Cotonou		Niamey	
	Yoruba	Hausa	Yoruba	Hausa	Yoruba	Hausa
Group % Yoruba	1	0	1	0	1	0
Group % Hausa	0	1	0	1	0	1
Group % Christian	0.56	0	0.27	0	0.12	0
Group % Muslim	0.44	1	0.73	1	0.88	1
Host % Yoruba	0	0	0.11	0.11	0	0
Host % Hausa	0	0	0	0	0.42	0.42
Host % Christian	0.98	0.98	0.74	0.74	0.008	0.008
Host % Muslim	0.01	0.01	0.13	0.13	0.99	0.99
Ethnic overlap	$(1*0)$ $+(0*0)$ $=0$	$(0*0)$ $+(1*0)$ $=0$	$(1*0.11)$ $+(0*0)$ $=0.11$	$(0*0.11)$ $+(1*0)$ $=0$	$(1*0)$ $+(0*0.42)$ $=0$	$(0*0)$ $+(1*0.42)$ $=0.42$
Religious overlap	$(0.56*0.98)$ $+(0.44*0.01)$ $=0.55$	$(0*0.98)$ $+(1*0.01)$ $=0.01$	$(0.27*0.74)$ $+(0.73*0.13)$ $=0.29$	$(0*0.74)$ $+(1*0.13)$ $=0.13$	$(0.12*0.008)$ $+(0.88*0.99)$ $=0.87$	$(0*0.008)$ $+(1*0.99)$ $=0.99$
Cultural overlap	0.275	0.005	0.20	0.065	0.435	0.705

C. List of Mass Expulsions and Variable Description

TABLE C.1. *List of Expulsions*

Country	Year	Number Affected	Primary Target
Republic of Congo	1962	130	Beninois
Niger	1963	8,000	Beninois
Côte d'Ivoire	1964	16,000	Beninois
Democratic Republic of Congo	1964	N/A	Congolese (Brazzaville)
Cameroon	1967	800	Nigerians
Senegal	1967	N/A	Guineans
Guinea	1968	N/A	Ghanaians
Côte d'Ivoire	1968	N/A	Ghanaians
Sierra Leone	1968	8,000	Ghanaians
Ghana	1969	500,000	Nigerians
Sierra Leone	1971	1,000	Guineans
Democratic Republic of Congo	1971	372	Nigerians
Zambia	1971	150,000	Zimbabweans
Uganda	1972	50,000	Asians
Democratic Republic of Congo	1972	Hundreds	Tanzanians
Democratic Republic of Congo	1972	Hundreds	Nigerians
Equatorial Guinea	1974	30,000	Nigerians
Sudan	1974	500	Nigerians
Equatorial Guinea	1976	N/A	Nigerians
Republic of Congo	1977	N/A	West Africans
Kenya	1977	N/A	N/A
Zambia	1977	400	N/A
Gabon	1978	9,000	Beninois
Democratic Republic of Congo	1978	N/A	Zambians
Chad	1979	N/A	Beninois
Kenya	1979	4,400	Tanzanians, Ugandans
Zambia	1979	4,000	Congolese (Kinshasa)
Kenya	1980	2,000	Tanzanians
Gabon	1982	5,000	Cameroonais

(continued)

TABLE C.I *(continued)*

Country	Year	Number Affected	Primary Target
Sierra Leone	1982	N/A	Foulah
Uganda	1982	N/A	Banyarwanda
Liberia	1983	N/A	N/A
Nigeria	1983	2,000,000	N/A
Uganda	1983	50,000	Rwandans
Djibouti	1984	N/A	Ethiopians
Côte d'Ivoire	1985	10,000	Ghanaians
Nigeria	1985	700,000	Ghanaians
Kenya	1989	N/A	Ugandans
Mauritania	1989	70,000	Senegalese
Senegal	1989	90,000	Mauritanians
Zambia	1992	517	West Africans
South Africa	1993	80,000	Mozambicans
South Africa	1994	90,000	Zimbabweans
Ethiopia	1998	N/A	Eritreans

TABLE C.2. *Variable List and Description for Difference-of-Means Analysis in Chapter 5*

Variable	Description	Source
Average population (*Thousands at mid-year*)	Average country population from independence to 1999	Maddison (2003)
Typical population density (*Persons/km²*)	Typical population density experienced by an individual	Harvard University CID (2009)
Area (*km²*)	Land area calculated in equal area projection	Harvard University CID (2009)
Immigrant population proportion (*Percentage*)	The number of immigrants as a proportion of the country's population in 2000	The World Bank (2011)
Absolute distance from equator (*Degree latitude*)	Absolute value of the latitude of a country's centroid	Harvard University CID (2009)
Land boundary (*Kilometers*)	Length land boundary	Central Intelligence Agency (2011a)
Percent arable land (*Percentage*)	Percentage of country's land that is arable	Central Intelligence Agency (2011a)
Percent mountainous (*Percentage*)	Percentage of a country's area that is mountainous	Fearon and Laitin (2003)
Jus sanguini (*Binary*)	Binary variable for whether the country has jus sanguini or jus soli citizenship laws	Herbst (2000)
French colony (*Binary*)	Colonized by the French	Fearon and Laitin (2003)
British colony (*Binary*)	Colonized by the British	Fearon and Laitin (2003)
Number of war years (*Count*)	Number of civil war years	Fearon and Laitin (2003)
Number of colonial war years (*Count*)	Number of liberation war years	Fearon and Laitin (2003)
ELF (*Index*)	Ethnolinguistic fractionalization	Fearon and Laitin (2003)
Plurality group size (*Percentage*)	Largest ethnic group's share of the population	Fearon and Laitin (2003)
Religious fractionalization (*Index*)	Religious fractionalization	Fearon and Laitin (2003)
Muslim population (*Percentage*)	Size of the Muslim population	Fearon and Laitin (2003)

Bibliography

Addo, N. O. (1982). Government-induced transfers of foreign nationals. In *Redistribution of Population in Africa*, pp. 31–38. London: Heinemann.

Adepoju, A. (1984). Illegals and expulsion in Africa: The Nigerian experience. *International Migration Review 18*(3), 426–436.

Afolayan, A. (1988). Immigration and expulsion of ECOWAS aliens in Nigeria. *International Migration Review 22*(1), 4–27.

Afrobarometer (2005). *Round 3 Ghana 2005 dataset*. Lansing, MI: Afrobarometer.

Alba, R. and V. Nee (2003). *Remaking the American mainstream; Assimilation and contemporary immigration*. Cambridge, MA: Harvard University Press.

Allport, G. W. (1954). *The nature of prejudice*. Cambridge, MA: Addison-Wesley.

Aluko, O. (1985). The expulsion of illegal aliens from Nigeria: A study in Nigeria's decision-making. *African Affairs 84*(337), 539–560.

Banerjee, A. V. and E. Duflo (2007). The economic lives of the poor. *The Journal of Economic Perspectives 21*(1), 141–168.

Barth, F. (1969). *Ethnic groups and boundaries*. Boston, MA: Little, Brown.

Beck, T., G. Clarke, A. Groff, P. Keefer, and P. Walsh (2001). New tools in comparative political economy: The database of political institutions. *World Bank Economic Review 15*(1), 165–176.

Blalock, H. M. (1967). *Toward a theory of minority-group relations*. New York: Wiley.

Blumer, H. (1958). Race prejudice as a sense of group position. *Pacific Sociological Review 1*(1), 3–7.

Bonacich, E. (1973). A theory of middlemen minorities. *American Sociological Review 38*, 583–594.

Brass, P. (1997). *Theft of an idol*. Princeton, NJ: Princeton University Press.

Brennan, E. M. (1984). Irregular migration: Policy responses in Africa and Asia. *International Migration Review 18*(3), 409–425.

Brewer, M. B. (2001). The psychology of prejudice: Ingroup love or outgroup hate? *Journal of Social Issues 55*(3), 429–444.

Burke, M., E. Miguel, S. Satyanath, J. Dykema, and D. Lobell (2009). Warming increases risk of civil war in Africa. *Proceedings of the National Academy of Sciences 106*(49), 20670–20674.

Burns, P. and J. Gimpel (2000). Economic insecurity, prejudicial stereotypes, public opinion on immigrant policy. *Political Science Quarterly 115*(2), 201–225.

Central Intelligence Agency (2011a). *CIA World Factbook*. Central Intelligence Agency. https://www.cia.gov/library/publications/the-world-factbook/.

Central Intelligence Agency (2011b). *CIA World Factbook: Niger*. Central Intelligence Agency. https://www.cia.gov/library/publications/the-world-factbook/geos/ng.html.

Challenor, H. S. (1979). *Strangers in African societies*, Strangers as colonial intermediaries: The Dahomeyans in Francophone Africa, pp. 67–83. Berkeley: University of California Press.

Chazan, N. (1982). Ethnicity and politics in Ghana. *Political Science Quarterly 97*(3), 461–485.

Chua, A. (2004). *World on fire: How exporting free market democracy breeds ethnic hatred and global instability*. New York: Anchor Books.

Citrin, J., D. P. Green, C. Muste, and C. Wong (1997). Public opinion toward immigration reform: The role of economic motivations. *The Journal of Politics 59*(3), 858–881.

Cohen, A. (1969). *Custom and politics in urban Africa*. London: Routledge and K. Paul.

Copnall, J. (2007). Xenophobia rules. *BBC Focus on Africa 18*(1), 14–15.

Cornelius, W. A., T. Tsuda, and Z. Valdez (2002). Human capital versus social capital: A comparative analysis of immigrant wages and labor market incorporation in Japan and the United States. Discussion Paper 476, Institute for the Study of Labor (IZA).

Daily Graphic (1969, December 5).

Dancygier, R. (2010). *Immigration and conflict in Europe*. New York: Cambridge University Press.

de Bruijn, M., R. van Dijk, and D. Foeken (Eds.) (2001). *Mobile Africa: Changing patterns of movement in Africa and beyond*. Leiden: Koninklijke Brill NV.

Deaton, A. (1998). *The analysis of household surveys: A microeconometric approach to development policy.* Baltimore The Johns Hopkins University Press.

Esses, V. M., L. M. Jackson, and T. L. Armstrong (1998). Intergroup competition and attitudes toward immigrants and immigration: An instrumental model of group conflict. *Journal of Social Issues 54,* 699–724.

Fafchamps, M. (2004). *Market institutions in Sub-Saharan Africa.* Cambridge, MA: MIT Press.

Fearon, J. D. (1999). Why ethnic politics and "pork" tend to go together. Working Paper presented at a conference on Ethnic Politics and Democratic Stability, Wilder House, University of Chicago, May 21–23.

Fearon, J. D. and D. D. Laitin (1996). Explaining interethnic cooperation. *American Political Science Review 90*(4), 715–735.

Fearon, J. D. and D. D. Laitin (2003). Ethnicity, insurgency, and civil war. *The American Political Science Review 97*(1), 75–90.

Forbes, H. (1997). *Ethnic conflict.* New Haven, CT: Yale University Press.

Geschiere, P. (2009). *The perils of belonging: Autochthony, citizenship, and exclusion in Africa.* Chicago: The University of Chicago Press.

Gomda, A. (2006, November 13). Discovering Accra: The making of the Zongos. *Daily Guide.*

Gradstein, M. and M. Schiff (2006). The political economy of social exclusion, with implications for immigration policy. *Journal of Population Economics 19*(2), 327–344.

Granovetter, M. (1973). The strength of weak ties. *American Journal of Sociology 78,* 1360–1380.

Granovetter, M. (1995). *Getting a job: A study of contacts and careers.* Chicago: University of Chicago Press.

Greif, A. (1993). Contract enforceability and economic institutions in early trade: The Maghribi traders' coalition. *The American Economic Review 83*(3), 525–549.

Gwatkin, D. R. (1972). Policies affecting population in West Africa. *Studies in Family Planning 3*(9), 214–221.

Haakonsen, J. M. (1991). *La recherche face à la pêche artisanale.* Paris: Orstom-Ifremer.

Hainmueller, J. and D. Hangartner (2013). Who gets a Swiss passport? A natural experiment in immigrant discrimination. *American Political Science Review 107*(1), 159–187.

Hainmueller, J. and M. J. Hiscox (2007). Educated preferences: Explaining attitudes toward immigration in Europe. *International Organization 61,* 399–442.

Harvard University CID (2009). Harvard University CID.

Henckaerts, J.-M. (1995). *Mass expulsion in modern international law and practice*, Volume 41 of *International studies in human rights*. The Hague: Martinus Nijhoff Publishers.

Herbst, J. I. (2000). *States and power in Africa: Comparative lessons in authority and control*. Princeton, NJ: Princeton University Press.

Himbara, D. and D. Sultan (1995). Reconstructing the Ugandan state and economy: The challenge of an international Bantustan. *Review of African Political Economy* 22(63), 85–93.

Horowitz, D. (1985). *Ethnic groups in conflict*. Berkeley: University of California Press.

Huntington, S. P. (1996). *The clash of civilizations and the remaking of world order*. New York: Simon and Schuster.

Igué, J. O. (2003). *Les Yoruba en Afrique de l'ouest francophone, 1910–1980*. Paris: Présence africaine.

Jalloh, A. (1999). *African entrepreneurship: Muslim Fula merchants in Sierra Leone*. Number 71 in Center for International Studies Monograph Series. Athens: Ohio University Center for International Studies.

Jeon, S. (2011). Middleman minorities and ethnic violence: The rational choice perspective. Stanford University Working Paper.

Jha, S. (2007). Maintaining peace across ethnic lines: New lessons from the past. *Economics of Peace and Security Journal* 2(2), 89–93.

King, G., M. Tomz, and J. Wittenberg (2000). Making the most of statistical analyses: Improving interpretation and presentation. *American Journal of Political Science* 44(2), 347–361.

Konings, P. (2001). Mobility and exclusion: Conflicts between autochthons and allochthons during political liberalisation in Cameroon. In M. de Bruijn, R. van Dijk, and D. Foeken (Eds.), *Mobile Africa: Changing patterns of movement in Africa and beyond*, Volume 1, 169–194. Leiden: Koninklijke Brill NV.

Laitin, D. D. (1986). *Hegemony and culture: Politics and religious change among the Yoruba*. Chicago: University of Chicago Press.

Laitin, D. D. (1994). The Tower of Babel as a coordination game: Political linguistics in Ghana. *American Political Science Review 88*, 622–634.

Laitin, D. D. (1995). Marginality: A microperspective. *Rationality and Society* 7(31), 31–57.

Laitin, D. D. (1998). *Identity in formation: The Russian-speaking populations in the near abroad*. Ithaca, NY: Cornell University Press.

Lalou, R., M. Ndiaye, and R. Nelly (1999). Facteurs d'attraction et de répulsion à l'origine des flux migratoires internationaux: Rapport National Sénégal. Technical Report 3/2000/E/n12, Institut de Recherche pour le Développement.

Lapinski, J. S., P. Peltola, G. Shaw, and A. Yang (1997). The polls-trends: Immigrants and immigration. *Public Opinion Quarterly 61*, 356–383.

Lefebvre, G. (2003). *Etre Etranger et Migrant en Afrique au XXe Siecle: Enjeux Identitaires et Modes d'Insertion*, Volume II, Chapter: La Communauté Guinéenne de Dakar, Une Intégration Réussie?, pp. 133–150. Paris: L'Harmattan.

Levine, R. A. and D. T. Campbell (1972). *Ethnocentricism: Theories of conflict, ethnic attitudes and group behavior*. New York: Wiley.

Lieberson, S. (1980). *A piece of the pie*. Berkeley: University of California Press.

Lipset, S. M. (1959). Some social requisites of democracy. *American Political Science Review 53*(1), 69–105.

Maddison, A. (2003). *The World Economy: Historical Statistics*. Development Centre Studies. Paris: OECD.

Malhotra, N., Y. Margalit, and C. H. Mo (2013). Economic explanations for opposition to immigration: Distinguishing between prevalence and magnitude. *American Journal of Political Science 57*(2), 391–410.

Manby, B. (2009). *Struggles for citizenship in Africa: A guide to knowledge as power*. London: Zed Books Ltd.

Marx, A. (1998). *Making race and nation: A comparison of the United States, South Africa, and Brazil*. Cambridge: Cambridge University Press.

Miguel, E., S. Satyanath, and E. Sergenti (2004). Economic shocks and civil conflict: An instrumental variables approach. *Journal of Political Economy 112*(4), 725–753.

Miles, W. F. S. and D. A. Rochefort (1991). Nationalism versus ethnic identity in sub-Saharan Africa. *The American Political Science Review 82*(2), 393–403.

Minorities At Risk Project (2003). *Minorities At Risk Project: Assessment for Ewe in Ghana*. www.cidcm.umd.edu/mar/assessment.asp? groupid=45202. Minorities At Risk Project.

Nyamnjoh, F. B. (2006). *Insiders and outsiders: Citizenship and xenophobia in contemporary southern Africa*. London: Zed Books Ltd.

Olzak, S. (1989). Labor unrest, immigration, and ethnic conflict in urban America, 1880–1914. *American Journal of Sociology 94*(6), 1303–1333.

Olzak, S. (1992). *The dynamics of ethnic competition and conflict*. Stanford, CA: Stanford University Press.

Ostien, P. (2009). Jonah Jang and the Jasawa: Ethno-religious conflict in Jos, Nigeria. Technical report, Volkswagen Stiftung.

Peil, M. (1971). The expulsion of West African aliens. *The Journal of Modern African Studies* 9(2), 205–229.

Peil, M. (1979). Strangers in African societies. In *Host reactions: Aliens in Ghana*, pp. 123–140. Berkeley: University of California Press.

Pellow, D. (1985). Muslim segmentation: Cohesion and divisiveness in Accra. *The Journal of Modern African Studies* 23(3), 419–444.

Portes, A. and R. G. Rumbaut (2001). *Legacies: The story of the immigrant second generation*. Berkeley: University of California Press.

Posner, D. N. (2004a). Measuring ethnic fractionalization in Africa. *American Journal of Political Science* 48(4), 849–863.

Posner, D. N. (2004b). The political salience of cultural difference: Why Chewas and Tumbukas are allies in Zambia and adversaries in Malawi. *The American Political Science Review* 98(4), 529–545.

Posner, D. N. (2007). Regime change and ethnic cleavages in Africa. *Comparative Political Studies* 40(11), 1302–1327.

Quillian, L. (1995). Prejudice as a response to perceived group threat: Population composition and anti-immigrant and racial prejudice in Europe. *American Sociological Review* 60(4), 586–611.

Rankin, M. B. (2005). Extending the limits or narrowing the scope? Deconstructing the OAU refugee definition thirty years on. New Issues in Refugee Research Evaluation and Policy Analysis Unit Working Paper No. 113.

Ricca, S. (1989). *International migration in Africa*. Geneva: International Labour Organization.

Rouch, J. (1956). Migrations au Ghana. *Journal de la Société des Africanistes* 26(1–2), 33–196.

Rumbaut, R. G. and A. Portes (2001). *Ethnicities: Children of immigrants in America*. Berkeley: University of California Press.

Schelling, T. (1978). *Micromotives and macrobehavior*. New York: Norton.

Sears, D. O. and J. B. McConahy (1973). *The politics of violence: The new urban blacks and the Watts riots*. Boston, MA: Houghton-Mifflin.

Shack, W. A. and E. P. Skinner (Eds.) (1979). *Strangers in African societies*. Berkeley: University of California Press.

Sise, L. J. (1975). *Expulsion of aliens in international law: Some African case studies*. Baltimore: Johns Hopkins University.

Sniderman, P., P. Pierangelo, R. de Figuerido, and T. Piazza (2000). *The outsider: Prejudice and politics in Italy*. Princeton, NJ: Princeton University Press.

Sniderman, P. M., L. Hagendoorn, and M. Prior (2004). Predisposing factors and situational triggers: Exclusionary reactions to immigrant minorities. *The American Political Science Review* 98(1), 35–49.

Sudarkasa, N. (1977). Women and migration in contemporary West Africa. *Signs* 3(1), 178–189.

Sudarkasa, N. (1979). *Strangers in African societies*. Berkeley: University of California Press.

Sulley, A. A. (2007). Hausa: Is it a Ghanaian language? *Bilingual Free Press*, 6.

Tajfel, H. (1981). *Human groups and social categories*. Cambridge: Cambridge University Press.

Tajfel, H. and J. C. Turner (1979). *The social psychology of intergroup relations*. Monterey, CA: Brooks-Cole.

Tajfel, H. and J. C. Turner (1986). *Psychology of intergoup relations*. Chicago: Nelson-Hall.

The World Bank (2011). The World Bank.

Tomz, M., J. Wittenberg, and G. King (2003, January). *CLARIFY: Software for interpreting and presenting statistical results. Version 2.1.* Stanford University, University of Wisconsin and Harvard University.

United Nations (2010, December). *United Nations Statistics Division – Standard Country and Area Codes Classifications*. United Nations.

Weiner, M. (1992–1993). Security, stability, and international migration. *International Security* 17(3), 91–126.

Weisberg, H. F. (2005). *The total survey error approach: A guide to the new science of survey research*. Chicago: The University of Chicago Press.

Wilkinson, S. I. (2006). *Votes and violence*. Cambridge: Cambridge University Press.

Woods, D. (2003). The tragedy of the cocoa pod: Rent-seeking, land and ethnic conflict in Ivory Coast. *The Journal of Modern African Studies* 41(4), 641–655.

Woolcock, M. (1998). Social capital and economic development: Toward a theoretical synthesis and policy framework. *Theory and Society* 27, 151–208.

Index